Wedding Speeches & Toasts

Pocket Guide to

Wedding Speeches

& Toasts

Darren Noel

G^E

This edition produced 2005 by
PRC Publishing,
The Chrysalis Building
Bramley Road, London W10 6SP

An imprint of **Chrysalis** Books Group plc

Published by Greenwich Editions
The Chrysalis Building
Bramley Road, London W10 6SP

An imprint of **Chrysalis** Books Group plc

ISBN 0 86288 630 9

Printed and bound in Malaysia

Contents

Introduction	6
Etiquette	9
Creating a Speech	19
Father of the Bride Speeches	47
Groom Speeches	70
Bride Speeches	106
Father of the Groom Speeches	120
Bridesmaid Speeches	125
Best Man Speeches	129
Toasts and Quotes	204
Appendix	232
Index	255

Introduction

*Y*our wedding day is the "happiest day of your life," and to live up to this expectation you want everything to run smoothly, especially the speeches and toasts. A great speech with the right amount of sentiment and humor will provide a memorable moment for everyone that attends. The *Pocket Guide to Wedding Speeches and Toasts* is an excellent guide to creating, writing, and delivering a speech you will feel proud of.

A wedding speech is a way of showing the affection you hold for the bride or groom, a way of saying thanks, and an opportunity to make a few toasts. If you are part of the happy couple, it is a chance to say thanks to those who have attended and give a personal message to your partner. To make a good speech, you do not need to have extensive experience of public speaking. No one is expecting you to be a comic genius, or to offer a slick presentation like a politician. It is all a matter of finding the right style for you and presenting it in a way that you find easiest and most comfortable.

The first section of the book includes some advice and tips on etiquette. Weddings have a lengthy history and traditions that have developed over time. This does not mean a wedding has to follow a strict code, but it is useful to be aware of any expectations, expecially for those making a speech. It is not a tradition for the female members of the wedding party to make a speech, but many now are choosing to do so. In fact it can be an advantage if there are no expectations as the bride or bridesmaids can feel freer to make the speech whatever they want it to be. The father of the bride, groom, and best man—the traditional wedding speakers—are, however, not so lucky. The father of the bride is expected to be sentimental about his daughter and the best man to give a character assasination of the groom in a speech that is entertaining and humorous. This is a daunting prospect for the speaker as he imagines a room full of people, expecting great things, ten minutes for him to keep the whole room entertained, and with little or no idea where to start.

This is where the next section, Creating a Speech, will help. It outlines where to start, how to do any research, and how to write your speech. It then goes on to offer tips and advice for delivering the speech and any preparation that is needed beforehand. There are many styles that a speaker may wish to adopt. Some choose to use visual props, involve some members of the audience in one or two jokes, or even to use slides during their speeches. Others choose to keep it simple, offering sentiment rather than entertainment.

Examples of actual speeches follow this section, which will give the reader inspiration on what to include in their own speech as well as ideas on presentation. There are examples where two speakers have spoken at the same time, or have included songs and poems in their speeches. There are others whose speeches are packed with jokey one-liners and some who have been quite sentimental. A few have found a balance between the two, delivering speeches that are both entertaining and affectionate.

My wife and I married in 1998. While I have presented to professional people and groups in the past, when it came to writing my own wedding speech, I was incredibly self-conscious. In addition to this, my best man, and the person who was giving my future wife away, were both very funny and incredibly confident people and I knew that their speeches were going to be very well received. Just the kind of pressure you don't need. With all of this in mind, I was determined that I would prepare and deliver a speech that would not disgrace my credibility among my family and friends. No one could have been more worried about giving a wedding speech than I was. Since then, I've read literally thousands of wedding speeches, listened to hundreds of speeches that have been recorded on video, and been contacted by various members of wedding parties asking for advice. In writing this book I aim to pass some of this knowledge onto you so that your big day can be as enjoyable as mine was.

$\mathcal{E}t\,i\,q\,u\,e\,t\,t\,e$

$\mathcal{W}$ eddings, no matter how formal or informal, follow some kind of etiquette. This is especially evident in the speeches that the various members of the wedding party make. Each speaker needs to know who to thank, when to present gifts, and if necessary how to give a toast. This section answers some of these questions.

$\mathcal{W}h\,o\;\;\mathcal{M}a\,k\,e\,s\;\;a\;\;\mathcal{S}p\,e\,e\,c\,h\,?$

The first thing to decide is if you really need to make a speech. A traditional wedding contains three speeches: the bride's father's speech, the groom's speech, and the best man's speech. No further speeches are required. However, it is not unusual, for example, for the groom's father to give a short speech of thanks to the host and hostess for the occasion. or the bride to have a "best woman" give a speech. In fact, nowadays, it is becoming more and more common for the bride herself to give a speech.

   If you do not fall into the category of bridegroom, best man, or father of the bride, except in exceptional circumstances, you shouldn't feel obliged to give a speech. On the other hand, if you are part of the immediate wedding party, you may feel that for one reason or another, you should say a few words. You may also have been asked by the bride or groom to speak on their behalf or on behalf of a loved one who cannot be at the wedding.

When to Deliver a Speech

More often than not, wedding speeches are given following the meal (usually just as coffee is being served). However, there are weddings where the groom, best man, or father of the bride is so nervous about speaking that they have decided to deliver the speeches prior to the meal. There are a number of positive or negative considerations to take into account if you are going to choose this as an option.

Delivering the speech prior to eating will probably make the dinner much more enjoyable for the speakers. Most of us find it difficult to eat when we are nervous. One of the problems often faced by grooms, best men, and fathers of the bride is that it is difficult to string a sentence together when you've had a few drinks. Delivering the speech prior to any eating or drinking ensures that the speaker is more coherent.

On the negative side, it is not traditional to give the speeches before the meal and while this may be acceptable to most of us, some may feel that delivering the speeches before the meal somehow takes away something from the big day. At the beginning of the meal, your audience will be less conducive to laughing at your jokes. In the absence of a professional warm-up act alcohol is often a good substitute! Whether right or wrong, alcohol (in reasonable quantities) can help put your audience in the right frame of mind. By the end of the meal, most of the audience will have had a drink or two and may well be slightly merry. While this may add some heckling to the speeches (which often adds to any humor), it will also ensure that the speeches are received by an audience that wants to laugh.

Duties of the Bride and Bridesmaids

The bride's work begins months in advance and doesn't stop even on the day itself. She has overall responsibility for coordinating just about every aspect of the wedding day. Although it is becoming more and more common for a bride to say a few words, she isn't expected to make a speech.

Age and marital status no longer come into who is chosen to be bridesmaid, usually the closeness of her relationship to the bride is a factor. The bridesmaid, especially a chief bridesmaid, is her trusted confidante and performs a similar role to that of best man for the groom. The bridesmaid organizes the hen night and, although not expected to, may give a speech.

Role of the Groom

The groom is given the task of choosing small gifts for the attendants and he usually presents these in his speech. The ushers are chosen by the groom and are usually brothers or cousins of the bride or groom.

Parents of the Bride and Groom

The mother of the bride travels to the wedding venue with the bridesmaids and is met at the entrance by the usher, who escorts her to her seat. The father of the bride travels with her to the wedding and walks by her side down the aisle. The parents of the bride are the official hosts of the reception and the mother of the bride is traditionally the first person to greet the arriving guests in the reception line. She does not make a speech, but it is the task of the father of the bride to do so and he usually is the first.

Traditionally, the groom's parents have played a more minor role. They are not expected to make a speech, but it is not exceptional for the father of the groom to deliver one.

Role of the Toastmaster

Prior to the day, the toastmaster should be made aware of who is giving the speeches, the order in which they are being given, and the time at which the speeches will be made. While a lot of venues supply their own toastmaster (or at least provide someone to act as the master of ceremonies) some do not. In this instance, to ensure that the day runs smoothly, there are two options that are available.

Firstly, the bridal party may see fit to arrange for their own toastmaster to be in attendance for the day. Toastmasters are professional people that will oversee the timing of the speeches and introduce the necessary people as and when required. The other more commonly used option, is for the best man to act as toastmaster—as if he hasn't got enough to worry about!

If you have been asked to be the best man, you will need to know if there will be a toastmaster present for the day. If not, the likelihood is that it will become one of your duties to act in a dual role and perform the relevant functions that the toastmaster would normally perform. As a toastmaster/best man there are several things you may be called upon to do.

Role of the Best Man

Prior to the ceremony (whether it be a religious or civil service), there is a very good chance that guests will be milling around outside the ceremony location just before it is due to begin. One of the best man's duties is to mingle with the guests and keep them entertained but as the toastman, you should also be in constant contact with the registrar, priest, vicar, or whoever it is that is performing the ceremony. While not interfering when it is not necessary, you should make it clear to them that you are the point of contact whom they can rely upon to make any announcements or direct people from one location to another when required. Remember that you are the groom's best man and it is your job to ensure that as much of the worry as possible is taken from the groom's shoulders. It is important that you also keep the groom up to date with any events that he should know about, but you should also be discreet when necessary. It is also important for any ushers that are in attendance to be kept up to date with what is happening. As best man, you are the person they should look to for guidance and you should ensure that they are in the right place at the right time to act as your supporters.

When called upon by the registrar, priest, vicar, or whoever it is that is performing the ceremony, you will need to make an announcement that will advise all of the guests to make their way into the church or ceremony room as required. The form that this announcement takes will vary depending on each individual set of circumstances, but something very short and to the point should suffice. One thing to remember at this point is that you are addressing your audience for the first time and, therefore, what you say now and how you say it may be remembered later in the day when it comes to your main speech.

As toastmaster, you need do nothing more until the end of the ceremony. You may find that at the end of the ceremony, you are called upon to direct the guests through to the reception room or to the area that has been designated as the reception area prior to the wedding breakfast. It is equally as likely that the registrar, priest, vicar, or whoever is performing the ceremony will give the instructions. In most circumstances, the next hour or so will be set aside for the wedding photographer to take the official photos of the wedding. During this period you will need to gather the relevant people together, as and when required. The photographs are usually followed by the receiving line, which generally leads into the room set aside for the wedding breakfast. As the best man, you are normally a part of this receiving line. As toastmaster, you are responsible for ensuring the guests are gathered together at the right place to meet the wedding party.

After all the guests have been through the receiving line, everyone should be in the dining room, seated, and ready to greet the bride and groom. As the toastmaster, your next task is to request that everyone is silent and standing ready to greet the bride and groom. Just prior to them entering the room, you should make a simple announcement:

> *"Ladies and Gentlemen, please stand and give your appreciation to*
> *the bride and groom—Mr. and Mrs. [their name]."*

Generally, as toastmaster you are not normally needed again until such time as the speeches are ready to begin. The exceptions to this are instances when short announcements may need to be made, such as advising of any smoking policy the venue has or possibly advising the guests of what they need to do in the case of an emergency evacuation of the building. If grace is to be said prior to the meal, it is often the responsibility of the toastmaster to do it, and it is best to have something written in advance. The toastmaster's next duty will be to introduce himself and then the other speakers.

Order of the Speeches

Nowadays, it is much more common for the female members of the wedding party to make a speech during the reception. If a bride/bridesmaid speech is going to be made, it is probably worth mentioning the order that the speaker would generally take. In most instances the following order of speakers would suffice:

* Father of bride
* Groom
* Bride
* Father of groom
* Bridesmaids/matron of honor
* Best man/woman

This order does not need to be stuck to rigorously. You may find that it is more suitable to switch this order around slightly, but it doesn't really matter what the order, so long as all the speakers are aware of who is saying what and when.

Traditionally, it is the bride's father who is called upon first. His speech is not normally expected to be a long or particularly humorous one, but speeches are a very personal thing and it is entirely up to the speaker to decide upon the content and the length of the speech. If you decide to follow tradition, and it is advisable to do this at least "loosely," the main part of this speech should consist of a number of points.

Firstly, the father of the bride would welcome the groom's parents, the relatives of both families, and then welcome all other guests. He would go on to propose a toast of "health and happiness to the bride and groom." To finish the speech, he would say a few words about his daughter. This section of the speech often takes the form of a humorous piece and then some deep and loving words are usually incorporated. At the end of this speech, the toastmaster should stand and introduce the groom.

The groom replies on behalf of himself and his wife, taking the opportunity to thank his parents for their love and care, for the start they gave him in life, and for their good wishes for his and his wife's future. He will also take this opportunity to thank all those present for their gifts.

It is customary for the groom to present the mother of the bride and the mother of the groom with a small gift. In the past, it would have been a bouquet of flowers, however it is now common for this gift to take the form of a keepsake (something such as an engraved silver bookmark or clock). While in gift-giving mode, the bride and groom often buy keepsakes for other direct members of the wedding party, such as the bridesmaids and ushers. The groom's speech is often used as the opportunity to present these gifts as well. Should there be any close members of the family who could not attend the wedding because of illness, they should be mentioned and wished a speedy recovery.

Once again humor is not necessary, however, as the groom you may wish to bear in mind that the best man is about to be given an opportunity to talk to a captivated audience about you. There is a very good chance that he will deliver a speech that (in the nicest way possible) totally ruins any credibility you have with your friends and family. This may be an opportunity of "warning" the audience about the best man's tendency to exaggerate stories and fabricate situations. Whether or not this makes any difference, it may make the groom feel better and raise a few laughs as well. To conclude, the bridegroom will propose the toast of the bridesmaids, and thank them for a job well done.

It is the best man's duty to respond to this toast on behalf of the bridesmaids. His speech should be lighthearted and fun and the high spot of the reception and it is very often his ability to make this particular speech, with humor and interest, which is the deciding factor on the selection of the best man. Apart from the humor, it is important that the best man also talks about his friendship with the groom and describes the qualities that the groom has that make him special. While he is expected to make a speech that is funny, he would also be expected to make a speech that will make the bride, the groom, and the wedding couple's family feel proud.

Creating a Speech

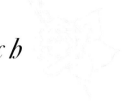

*W*hether you are the bride, groom, father of the bride, or the best man, making a speech may be one of the highlights of your role at the wedding. This section gives advice and tips on how to create a speech that is structured, follows the wedding etiquette, and sets the right tone for the audience that you will be addressing. It also gives advice on the delivery of your speech and any preparation that is needed beforehand.

Structure

One of the things that will make writing a speech easier is to think of a structure and use it when you start to write or do your research. Every speech, no matter how informal, will follow some kind of logical structure, which also makes it easier to deliver on the day. A basic outline that can be used as a speech template is as follows:

1. Opening lines
2. Comments on the service
3. Congratulations and thanks
4. Your relationship with the bride/groom
5. Some words about the stag do/hen night, if applicable

6. Anecdotes, stories, and reminiscences about the groom's/bride's past
7. Comments on the bride and groom's romance
8. Some compliments for the bride
9. Tributes to the groom
10. Advice for the bride and groom
11. Reading out cards and telegrams (usually done by the best man)
12. Closing lines
13. Toasts

To start with, think of your opening lines. These will set the tone and make a first impression on your audience, so they are in a way the most important. They are also the lines that you should learn by heart to start you off with confidence, before needing to refer to your notes for the rest of the speech. There are several things to include. First of all, introduce yourself to those members of the audience who may not know you. If the tone of your speech is humorous then perhaps add a joke to break the ice.

Next you can comment on the service; the bride and groom's outfits; and possibly the weather. This will bring you on to a necessary part of the speech, which is giving thanks, presenting gifts, and offering congratulations. Some speakers may also want to mention those who are absent at this point, as a way of remembrance. Best men usually thank the groom for choosing them, and perhaps the bride for agreeing to it. The best man also offers thanks from the bridesmaids as they may not get to make a speech of their own. The bride or groom thanks any helpers and the principal members of the wedding party. In fact you can thank anyone you think is appropriate and offer gifts at this point. Sometimes gifts are offered by the groom to the bridesmaids and other direct members of the family.

Before you go on to tell any anecdotes or stories you may have, describe your relationship with the bride or groom. You may be a friend from university, a work colleague, an old school friend, a sister, brother, or father. You could describe how you came to be friends if you are not a member of the family; how long you have known them; and your first impressions of them. This is not only a rich source of witty commentary, but a way of letting the audience get to know your relationship with the bride or groom, so that they can relate to any stories you may tell later on. What were your earliest memories of the bride or groom? If you knew him or her at school, what were they like? For the best man, even if you didn't know them as a child, you could still give a history of their early childhood (this is also mentioned as part of the research you will be doing later on in this section). Some best men include one-liners about the groom's past interests, fashion sense, bad habits, and appearance.

Best men or bridesmaids/maids of honor can at this point of the speech mention the stag party or hen night. Many best men usually allude to the fact that the groom misbehaved or is paying the speaker not to say anything. This is a way for the speaker to build up to the main part of the speech, which for the best man is usually an embarassing story or anecdotes about the groom.

If you are not giving a best man speech, you may still want to include a story about the bride or groom as the main part of your speech. Usually one story is enough; at a typical reception half the guests don't know the other half and the speech must be entertaining even to those who have never known the people you mention. If as a best man you choose to make a humorous speech, make sure it also includes an equal number of congratulatory remarks or some sentiment to show the regard that you hold for the bride and groom. Merely offering a speech full of jokes may not show the real affection that you have for them. Also bear in mind that weddings are an emotional time, so it may be more difficult to deliver a speech full of sentiment than you imagine. Striking the balance between offering some humor for entertainment and showing some sentiment is perhaps the best position to aim for as a best man.

After any anecdotes or reminiscences you may tell, you can comment on the bride and groom's romance. If you were there when they first met, how was it? What were their first impressions of each other? How did the relationship blossom? If you weren't a witness to any of this, you may like to say how the bride has made an impact on the groom's life. What are their expectations of marriage? You can give examples of their unique relationship. Comment on how happy they are and offer some optimistic remarks for the future.

Now you are getting to the latter stages of the speech you can begin to wrap up. Offer complimentary words about the bride and how she will make the groom a lovely wife. Say some tributes for the groom: congratulate him on marrying such a lovely bride; say what a good friend/brother/son he has been. Many speakers at this point offer some advice for the bride and groom. This is usually in the form of a few humorous comments.

The best man reads out cards and telegrams toward the end of his speech before his closing lines. This is an opportunity to mention those that were unable to attend the wedding and offer their congratulations. It is also an opportunity for the best man to add a few last joke cards of his own.

To end your speech, you may want to give a humorous summary, read out a poem, or even quote from a song (some speakers have even played a song). And last but not least, you can follow the speech by offering toasts, usually ending with a toast to the bride and groom.

Now that you have thought about the structure of your speech, you can do any research necessary before going on to write it. You can also try reading through some of the example speeches shown later in this book. As well as general inspiration, you may find some useful lines that you can use in your own speech or even a good joke or two that you think would be appropriate to include.

Research

Research may sound like a tedious word, but it's necessary if you want to create a good speech, especially for the best man or father of the bride. Here the best man's speech is used as an example and assumes that the speaker is starting with a blank sheet of paper. Over the period of time the best man has known the groom, there will have been hundreds of occasions when they laughed in each other's company. There must be many funny stories to tell and a wedding speech provides the ideal opportunity.

First of all get a notebook, preferably one with a hard cover, as the last thing you want is for someone (especially the groom) to get hold of your research or your final speech. To ensure your speech will be kept secret, make a hole through the book, from cover to cover, in the center on the right hand side, and then you can simply lock the book by using a small padlock. While this won't guarantee that nobody sees your research, it will discourage opportunist snooping. Use this book as your speech scrapbook. Every time you come across the slightest snippet of information, jot it down in the book. While the final speech may well be written on a computer, your book is by far the easiest way of gathering together all of the information you need to create a perfect speech.

Give yourself a few hours to make a start. During these early stages, it is advisable to briefly map out the groom's life. There are bound to be a lot of details that you do not know, but it probably will not be until you begin this task that you realize how many spaces there are in your knowledge.

Start with his birth date, including the day of the week. The smallest detail may prove useful later, as happened in one best man's speech:

> *"There is absolutely no truth to the rumor that Maurice (the groom)*
> *was named after the car in whose back seat he was conceived*
> *(Morris Minor). Had that been the case, he would actually have*
> *been named '23' as that was the number of the bus that ran*
> *between Mr. and Mrs. Smiths' (groom's parents) houses when they*
> *were courting."*

He later mentioned that that line came to him when he wrote the number twenty-three down as this also happened to be part of the groom's birth date.

Continue with his early years, his first words, his age when he began to crawl and then walk. His early birthday presents. Did he have a dummy? Did he suck his thumb, cry a lot, dislike certain foods, or people?

When did he first go to school? What was the name of his first teacher? What was the name of his first friend? Did he have a girlfriend in his infant years?

What about junior high school? Did he have an aptitude for anything during his early school years? Was he good at sport? Did any teachers take a shine to him? Were there any more girlfriends?

Then there was senior school. This is where things can often start to get more interesting. What subjects did he study at school? Was there a subject he particularly excelled in? Was there a subject he constantly received poor marks in? Can you find his old school reports? If there is something particularly juicy here, perhaps you can track down one of his old teachers? Did he play truant? Get in trouble? Any early brushes with the law? What about school trips, where, when, who with? Early dress sense and hairstyles. Gather some photographs. Any strange hobbies or pastimes? Did he own a teddy bear? Does he still own it?

After gathering information on his early life, which should provide lots of material, move on to his more formative years. When did he first leave home? Perhaps he went to college or university. Were there tears of sorrow or joy when he left? Where did he go and what did he study? What effect did his location or the subjects that he studied have on his life now? Any early loves? Was he a Romeo or a bit of a recluse? Was this his first introduction to the fine art of alcohol consumption? Try and find some early stories of him getting drunk and find pictures to go with them.

When this source of inspiration is exhausted, move on to his first few jobs. Maybe there were part-time jobs before he left school or college. Did he do a paper round? Was he a shop assistant? Did he work in a fast food restaurant? Any part-time work as a barman? What was his first real job? Did he stay doing it long? Is he still doing the same thing? Any promotions or demotions? Ever been fired? Has he ever done something disastrous and got in trouble for it? Better still, has he ever blamed someone else and got away with it? What relationship is there between his first job and his current position? What's happened in between?

Now for the really interesting part. Find out everything you can about his past relationships, but obviously use tact and choose examples that happened a long time ago, so that he won't feel too sensitive about it. Has he had his heart broken at school or was he a heart breaker? What happened in the lead up to meeting his bride? How long did they court? Did anyone predict it would end in marriage? Did anyone think it was a flash in the pan? How did they meet? Who made the early running? Was it love at first sight or did they grow to fall in love with one another? Any hiccups? Any early comments made by either the bride or groom that later came back to haunt them? You may also wish to use your scrapbook to collect pictures, love letters, school reports, or anything else that you come across. Once you gather all this information together, you will have the foundations for creating an excellent wedding speech.

Writing the Speech

Writing your speech is probably going to take the most time and it is extremely unlikely that you will complete it in a single sitting. You will also undoubtedly change it many, many times before you feel it is right. Don't feel at all disheartened if you sit down and after an hour or so of trying you have achieved very little. Sometimes, when trying to write a speech or anything else of this nature, your mind may go blank and you struggle to string a decent sentence together. If this happens, it is often better to leave it for a while and go back to it at another time. You may find that when you return to it, it begins to flow more naturally and you suddenly have half of the speech written before you know it.

Knowing the structure of your speech makes writing it much easier and with all the research that you have collected there will be plenty of material for you use. You may find that rather than being unable to write the speech, you find it is too long! If this is the case don't worry. Write everything that you think you want to include and then leave it for a few days. After a break from it you will be able to go back to it and edit it down, rewriting the parts that you now think are not so relevant. It is easier to cut things down than to try and expand on a meagre amount of words.

You will also find that when you come to practicing delivering the speech that you may want to leave things out or rewrite them. This is all part of the process, so don't expect to get it right in just one go.

Using Humor in a Speech

Some of the worst speeches are created by the speaker trying to be too funny. Making the audience cringe is bad enough, but if rude or inappropriate jokes are told there is a very good chance that while some of the audience may see the funny side, other members of the wedding party may take offense. The key to knowing how far you can go when telling jokes or funny stories lies in the audience. You really need to be sure that what you are going to say is not going to upset anyone. Aunty Edna's sense of humor is probably very different to cousin Bob's. If there is a danger that a joke or story may cause offense, it is better to play safe and remove it. Also avoid using any swear words for the same reason.

How Long Should a Speech Be?

One of the most commonly asked questions about wedding speeches is how long it should last. There is no right and wrong answer but as a rough guide, you should plan for each speech to last about ten to fifteen minutes. You will probably find that if you do plan a speech this long, on the day it will generally take a few minutes longer to deliver. In general, your speech should be long enough to entertain without being too long that it bores people.

Using Props and Visual Aids

If during your research you happen to come across pictures or any other visual aids, hold on to them for later use. You may find that you can use them as props during your speech. Props are becoming more and more common during wedding speeches, taking many forms and used in various ways.

You may wish to distribute certain items before you start your speech so that the guests are able to view them close up. For items such as letters and photographs, you can get them copied and place them in sealed envelopes on the tables with the inscription "do not open." Other items may be better used if they are copied and then enlarged for you to show during your speech. If you want to get really high-tech you may find that the venue can provide you with an overhead projector so that you can create a slide show for your audience. If you have some good images, this can be a very effective way of showing them.

You can also make use of guests at the wedding—so that they become the props. An excellent best man speech, shown later in this book, uses a spoof letter and some unexpected guests. If used in the right situation, old clothes that were once considered fashionable are also very valuable.

Preparation and Delivery

The research has been done, you know what you have to do on the day, and you have finally finished writing the speech, now you've just one thing left to worry about and that's the actual delivery of the speech on the day.

To some, both the thought of delivering a speech and the actual act of delivering it results in no nerves whatsoever. To others, having each hair of their eyebrows plucked individually by a masochist with a pair of pliers is a more appealing thought. There are a lot of steps you can take beforehand to ensure the delivery of the speech is easier when the time comes.

The first thing to do is make sure that you have gathered together any props well ahead of time. If you have to rely on others to bring certain items along with them, ensure that you remind them frequently and do everything you can to try and get those items in your hand well before the day.

If the speech is going to involve the audience and you need some of them to actually participate in the delivery, make sure that the individuals concerned are happy to be involved, are briefed in advance, and they know what they are supposed to do and when to do it. Involving members of the audience in your speech is an excellent way of ensuring they are kept entertained and can also be a good way of introducing humor. The one thing to bear in mind is that you should be careful not to alienate certain members or sections of the audience by constantly referring to individuals, groups, or stories that are not relevant or able to be understood by all of the guests.

On the day of the speech itself, you must ensure that you advise the venue manager, or other appropriate person, if you need anything from them. Make this one of your priorities on the morning of the wedding. Some things obviously won't be able to be arranged on the day and should have been planned ahead of time. For this reason there may be instances when you will have needed to contact the relevant person at the venue well before the day itself. Most venue managers will be happy to help, as it is in their interest that the day should go without a hitch—this will reflect well on the venue and them individually.

The biggest thing to remember, however, is to practice the speech over and over again. While you are writing the speech you will no doubt continually read it to yourself as you write, amend, and correct paragraphs. Once you have finished the first draft of it you will probably also read it again from beginning to end and then begin to make some more changes. Once you have written the final first draft, lock yourself away somewhere that you cannot be heard and read the speech out loud, as if you were delivering it on the day itself. After the first reading, you will probably find that you want to make changes yet again.

Your next task should be reading it out loud once again, but this time you should record the time it takes for you to deliver the speech. Try recording the speech so that you can play it back to yourself and hear what it sounds like. It's not until you actually hear the speech for yourself that you will really appreciate what it sounds like. The other thing to mention is that the length of time the speech takes you to deliver in practice will probably increase by a few minutes when it actually comes to delivering it on the day. This is obviously due to interruptions, applause, laughter (hopefully), and heckling that will probably come from the audience on the day itself.

When practicing your speech, one of the key things to remember is to speak at a regular tempo. One of the biggest and most common mistakes people make when they are giving a speech is that they speak too fast. Don't be afraid to pause every now and again if you feel it is necessary, or if you need to take a drink (or more importantly a breath).

When making a speech of any sort, very few people memorise it word for word and subsequently deliver it without referring to some notes or an autocue. With that in mind, you should not feel the need to memorise all of your speech. By reading it time and time again, you will probably find that when it comes to the time for delivering it, some of it will simply flow from memory and you will not have to refer to your notes too often.

There is, however, a down side to this. During the delivery of your speech, if at times you do find that it begins to flow from memory, you still need to refer to your notes frequently and ensure that, as the speech moves from one page to another, the new page is always on the top of your pile. There are a couple of reasons for this.

Firstly, while you will probably remember the main points and lines of the speech, there is a good chance that you may forget something that is of high importance. Keeping the current page on the top of the pile will allow you to glimpse at it constantly so that you are less likely to miss an important point. Secondly, if you find yourself halfway through a story or sentence and suddenly forget the next line, you will need to refer back to your notes. If you haven't looked at them for some time, you will find yourself frantically scrambling about through your notes for the relevant page and paragraph.

The one other thing worth mentioning now is the format the notes for your speech take. You can use the complete speech as your notes, but this is obviously a personal thing and while you are practicing the delivery of the speech you may find that this is not suitable for you.

Another option is to use cue cards—cards with notes on them that are used for reference and are small enough to fit into an inside pocket or in your hand while you are delivering the speech. For a more complicated option, you may find that an autocue is available. An autocue is an electronic system that projects your speech into a form that is visible to you but nobody else. When you see a politician making a speech you will often notice a couple of clear plastic sheets positioned just below eye level in front of them. These are autocue boards and the speech is automatically projected on to them. However, if you have never used this type of system before it may complicate things even further.

If you use the complete speech as your notes, break the speech down into sections. The size of these sections or the time each section will take to deliver may vary, however each of the sections will have a definite start and end point. Keep each section on a separate page so that you know as soon as you come to the end of that section that you don't even have to look at the page, you can simply turn over and the next section is clearly seen.

Give each section a heading or reference so that it acts as a prompt as soon as you turn over the page. Highlight the heading at the top of the page and show it in very large font, or even in a different color. Frequently, the reference or heading is enough for you to remember exactly what that section is about and you subsequently rarely have to refer to your notes.

The following speech, reproduced with the permission of Graeme Trotter, is included as an example. As you will see, it is broken down into sections and each section has a heading. The first section, entitled "Grand Opening" allows the speaker to introduce himself and also include his first gag to break the ice. The second section ensures that he thanks all the people that he needs to and congratulates the bride and groom. This may also be an opportunity for the speaker to present gifts, if necessary. Prompts are also given in brackets for when to initiate applause, or even when to pause for a reaction. The main part of the speech includes any stories about the groom and any advice that he may have for the happy couple. This is followed, of course, by the toasts.

Grand Opening

Ladies and Gentlemen, bride and groom. For those of you who do not know me my name is Graeme Trotter. It is a great honor to be chosen as Simon's best man today. And if I do a good job he's told me I can be best man at the next one.

This is probably the most terrifying ordeal that can be inflicted on anyone. I can assure you all that this is not the first time today that I have stood up from a warm seat with paper in my hand. It's great to be back at a normal wedding. Last week I attended one where two aerials got married. It was a dreadful wedding but the reception was great!

Thank-yous

Please allow me to officially congratulate the bride and groom. I think we all agree that the bride looks like one in a million today and that the groom has found someone not only gorgeous, but also intelligent, sophisticated, trustworthy, and patient. And in return, well, I cannot think of a better guy, a girl could marry.

> *[await reaction]*

With the exception of me.

> May I congratulate the families of those concerned. They have done a splendid job in making today a very emotional event.

> *[initiate applause]*

> On behalf of the bridesmaids, I'm sure you'll agree that they have done a wonderful job today and they look absolutely dazzling. Let's show our appreciation for the bridesmaids.

> *[initiate applause]*

The Main Stage

As this is the first time I've been a best man I discovered that I had a *number* of important duties to undertake:

1. Check that the groom is well looked after the night before. I have to say that after a couple of beers last night he told me he slept like a baby.

   [Pause]

   He woke up every hour crying for his mom.

2. Ensure that the groom is dressed properly.

   Well, he only has to look at me, minus the head.

3. Protect the groom from angry ex-girlfriends.

   The sheep epidemic helped me out with that one.

4. And finally, stop him from doing a runner.

The groom is three months younger than myself. Over time he has provided us with plenty of ammunition for this day, although not a lot of it legal. I would like to share a few of his more memorable moments with you.

I first met him thirteen years ago while at college. I knew his first girlfriend and I thought they would make a go of it until the day he over-inflated her. I had the pleasure of playing in a rock band with him for five years. I was always struck with how enthusiastic he was about playing his drums. He wasn't always so slick, however, as his hyperactiveness often got the better of him, leading to several broken drums, not to mention our ear-drums.

In 1990, the Vixens was a band with four of the greatest, sexiest girls ever to walk the planet—God bless them— and I discovered they had released a video. Determined to get this we both had a wander along to the music shop the following day. A few yards from the entrance the groom decided to run into the shop ahead of me to ensure he got the only copy on sale… *[look at him]* …the little rat. Imagine my delight when he ran straight past it. Cool as I could—I walked up and picked it off the shelf. Revenge was sweet when I taunted him for a little before handing over my money at the counter.

Though born and brought up in England, the groom is no stranger to Scotland. Only this morning a neighbor said to me, I have seen no stranger man in the whole of Scotland.

[Read out cards]

Wrap Up

A few things to remember for the future… and I'd like to ask the bride and groom to participate with this. *[To the bride]* If I can ask you to place your hand flat on the table… *[demonstrate]* O.K. *[To the groom]* If you would place your hand directly on top of the bride's. Enjoying that? Make the most of it, pal, it's the last time you'll have the upper hand.

Other things to take with you:

1. *[To the groom]* Remember the key to a happy marriage is to remember those three little words: "You're right dear."

2. Marriage is not only an eight-letter word, it is a sentence for life… and you can get a lesser sentence for murder, you know.

3. The best way to remember your wedding anniversary is to forget it once.

4. *[To the groom]* Always stand up for yourself. It doesn't matter if a thousand disagree or ten disagree, so long as the mother-in-law agrees with you.

5. And one more thing. Never take advice from anyone, particularly if that person is older than yourself. Now take my advice and don't take it.

And finally, ladies and gentlemen, it gives me immense pleasure to ask you to join me in a toast to the bride and groom. *[Raise glasses]* They have been on several adventures together; let this marriage be their greatest adventure yet.

Once you are happy with both your speech and the delivery of it, it is time to find yourself a good friend to act as a guinea pig. While you do not want many people to hear your speech before the big day, it is important to test the speech on a trial audience (even if that audience consists of just a single person.) Obviously the person that you select is entirely up to you, however there are three main qualities they should possess:

> *Discretion*: You do not want details of your speech reaching other people's ears so you must choose somebody who will keep the contents of your speech confidential.
> *Honesty:* You want somebody who will give you an honest opinion of the speech, so select somebody that will give you a constructive and candid opinion of the speech without knocking your confidence.
> *Experience*: If you are able to select somebody who has made a speech before, they may be able to advise you on certain lines or stories that could be delivered in a better way.

You should deliver the speech to them in exactly the same way you are planning on delivering it on the big day. You may feel embarrassed about delivering your speech in this fashion, however this is an excellent way of getting a good feel for how well your speech is going to be received on the day itself. Following the initial reading of the speech, you should ask your "guinea pig" for feedback. Ask for their honest overall opinion of the speech then break it down, a paragraph at a time, and ask for any specific comments about that particular section. The final question to ask them is about the actual delivery. Did you speak clearly, was the tempo of the speech consistent, were there too many words repeated (phrases like "you know" and "errm" are very often overused when making a speech).

Bear in mind that jokes you hope will be met with raptures of laughter may only raise a smile from your "guinea pig." This is absolutely nothing to worry about. People tend to laugh much more when in a group than in a one to one situation, where a smile is much more common.

Remember that you have asked this friend for their opinion because you need feedback from another person and you also trust their opinion. For this reason, you shouldn't get defensive if there is any criticism of your speech. Take criticism in a constructive way and try to hear what they are saying from their point of view. Remember, they are giving you this feedback to help you and anything they have to say should be listened to and at least given thoughtful consideration.

The final point to mention about delivery could make a difference between a good and a bad speech. One of the biggest mistakes you can make is to not make eye contact with your audience and/or show any gestures. A speech can be really enhanced if you make the right eye contact at the right time. If you simply read from a sheet of paper while remaining seated without looking up very often at all, no matter how good the content of the speech, it will be remembered more for the bad delivery as opposed to the good content.

Here are a few tips on body language and eye contact:

Always stand to deliver a speech:
This will ensure that your audience remain focused on you and what you are saying. The better their concentration on you, the more chance you have of delivering a well received speech.

Speak with confidence:
No matter how nervous you may feel, if you can deliver the opening line, phrase, or joke with confidence the better it will be received and therefore the more confident you will feel. For this reason, the opening line is the most important line of the speech and should be practiced time and time again until you are confident that you can stand and deliver it without any reference to your prompt sheets.

Eye contact:
When reciting a story about a particular person, continue to scan your focus across the members of the

audience and the wedding party. However, it is good practice to constantly return your eye contact to the individual who is the focus of the story. Additionally, when making any sentimental comments, they will be received with more meaning if you make eye contact with the relevant person.

Move around:

You do not have to stand in a stationary position when delivering your speech. However, neither should you constantly walk around the room when speaking, otherwise you run the risk of people constantly having to turn their heads to focus on you. If you feel that it is necessary to walk among your audience, by all means do so. You should also feel comfortable using your hands, arms, and any other part of your body (within reason) to demonstrate actions as and when necessary.

Don't whisper:

A good audience will tell you if they can't hear you but not all audiences are good. For this reason it is often a good idea to ask early in the speech if everyone can hear you. You should ensure that when you are delivering the speech it is delivered in a voice that is loud enough for all to hear without actually shouting.

To drink or not to drink:

That is definitely the question and the answer varies according to each individual. Just a glass or two of wine helps to calm your nerves. The worst thing you can do, however, is to go to stand to make your speech and then realize that your legs are a little wobbly. While falling flat on your back may generate a few early laughs, trying to deliver the speech from that position will be fairly difficult. Slurring your words is a definite no, especially at a wedding reception. During your speech ensure that you have a drink of some sort (not necessarily alcoholic) to hand for two reasons. Firstly you may wish to take a sip to clear your throat during your speech. Secondly, when it comes to toasts, you will need to raise a glass.

After the Speech

Time to breathe a sigh of relief. All the planning, research, writing, practicing, re-writing, learning, trying out, more practicing, more re-writing, and nerves are over. You can sit back, watch others speak, and feel very pleased with yourself. If everything has gone according to plan, at this point in the proceedings you may very shortly begin to receive thanks and congratulations from many members of the audience.

You may also feel a little sad. While the whole process of writing and delivering a speech at a wedding can be quite an ordeal, once you have actually finished delivering it, you'll probably want to do it all over again. It's a little like watching you favorite team finish the season by winning the big cup. You are anxious in the lead up to the final game, keen to see the game finish in a victory, however as soon as it is over with you'd like to go through all the anxiety again because deep down you really enjoyed the experience.

So what now? Enjoy the rest of the day. Weddings are amazing experiences for all concerned and even though the main part of your day may be over, the rest of the day is yours to enjoy.

Father of the Bride Speeches

⟨⎯⎯⎯⟩

A ny speech, whether short or long, is equally important and may need some forethought and inspiration before the big day. Depending on your individual circumstances, this and the following sections may possibly be the most useful part of this book. Reading through the examples that follow, you will see many speeches that have been successfully delivered at weddings all over the world. You may find one that strikes a chord and gives you a few ideas for your own speech. Whatever tone you bring to your speech, whether humorous, sentimental, or just a way to say congratulations and thankyou, is entirely up to you. You will see that speakers are not afraid to "borrow" a joke or a few lines from speeches they have read or heard before. How they deliver their speech and make it relevant to the bride and groom and the other guests is what makes the difference.

Fathers of the bride are traditionally the first to give a speech, which is why they are included in this first section. They don't normally have a lot to do with the planning of the wedding, but instead spend most of the actual day worried about what will become of their daughter. Then there's the small matter of keeping the guests occupied and interested while they make a speech that is somehow expected to be great.

All the speeches in this section are good examples to follow (all names have been removed). Some are very sentimental, which is perhaps what you would expect from a father of the bride speech, but others are very funny, which for some speakers is preferable, keeping sentiment for more private conversations. Included in this section is a speech by a bride's brother, in the absence of their father and an older sister, who performed the duties traditionally made by the father of the bride. It illustrates that this kind of speech can be delivered by other members of the family and there is no reason to be bound by tradition.

Father of the Bride–Example 1

The following speech was written, delivered by and reproduced with the kind permission of Chris Haywood.

It was written and performed by a father of the bride who was in the unenviable position of giving away his second daughter in less than a year. Writing one father of the bride speech is hard enough but two in such a short period of time must be very difficult. The speech is peppered with humorous lines and is an especially good example for someone who might prefer to keep the sentiment on a personal, one to one level.

This speech uses quotes that are skillfully woven into his more personal message, which is a good way of adding humor and providing the speaker with material that is neither offensive or dull. He also includes several jokes that are popular in wedding speeches, but has given his own twist on them to add originality.

Ladies and gentlemen, may I start my speech by welcoming the guests. Today, we are surrounded by most of the friends and family that have been important to us during our lives. Some have traveled thousands of miles, just to be here today. We welcome you all and thank you sincerely for sharing this special day with us.

As about half of you will know, this is my second father of the bride speech in less than a year. To misquote Oscar Wilde from *The Importance of*

Being Ernest: "To lose one daughter may be considered unlucky. To lose two is careless!" Well, I guess that's O.K. because my being careless is how they came to be here in the first place.

Making the father of the bride speech, I feel a bit like a Sheik walking into his harem for the first time. I know what I've got to do, I just don't know where to start. You will all be pleased to learn that my speech will be every bit as good as last time. In fact, my side of the family will probably remember great chunks of it. Not really, although I am following exactly the same format. This means it will probably start off badly, sag in the middle with long silences, and then trail off into a lot of incoherent rambling.

To be honest, I did try to memorize this speech, but forgive me if I resort to my notes every five seconds. I asked for an autocue to be set up in front of me. Apparently, the wedding budget doesn't stretch that far, and neither does my eyesight.

[To the groom] We are delighted to welcome you into the family. By now, you must be wondering what on earth you have let yourself in for. I want you to know that my wife and I took to you instantly. You are a kind and considerate man who deserves a good wife. Thank goodness you married *[the bride]* before you found one.

I am only kidding, of course. There is nothing in the world to match the thrill of seeing your first child born. She was a beautiful baby. She still is beautiful—in every sense of the word—and she has continued to fill our lives with happiness and pride.

Everyone knows that she is a rolling stone and couldn't wait to leave home and find new adventures at university. Since then she has made many firm friends, some of whom are decidedly odd, but I'll say no more about that because most of the odd ones seem to be here today.

Now where was I? I expect you may have noticed that the groom's getting on a bit—a few gray hairs already—so it's obviously taken him some time to find his Miss Right. In fact, his best man tells me he once sent his picture off to a Lonely Hearts Club. Apparently they sent it back, with a note saying they weren't that lonely.

The groom is a rugby player, or so I am told. I took time to ask some of his mates how good he was and where was his best position. To cut a long story short, he seems to be terrible in every position! I'm sure there's a joke there somewhere, but never mind.

The bride and groom are extremely well suited, aren't they? They're happy and they love each other. That should be enough to see them through life together. It has been said that marriage is a 50/50 partnership. Whoever said that knows nothing about women and even less about fractions.

I asked the groom recently what he was looking for in marriage. He said love, happiness, and eventually a family. I asked my daughter the same question. She replied "a coffee percolator." She actually said a "perky copulator," but I knew what she meant.

As you all know, fathers of the bride get to make the first speech. To be honest, it's a bit like being invited to sleep with the Queen Mother. It's a great honor, but you really don't want to do it! And what about the brides-maids? Didn't they look lovely, in the church? Having seen all the ushers, I thought for a minute I'd accidentally wandered onto the set of *Seven Brides for Seven Brothers*.

I started planning this speech a month ago—and you must feel like I've been delivering it equally as long—and I haven't quite finished yet because my next toast is to the bride and groom. That reminds me of the wedding I once went to where the two of the guests were a minister and a priest. When the priest was offered a drink for the toast he said "I'll have a large whisky please." When the minister was offered the same, he said "No thanks. I'd rather go with a scarlet woman than touch the demon alcohol." The priest promptly put his whisky back on the tray and said "I didn't know there was a choice."

Now I don't want to offend anybody, so if there's a priest or a minister present, I apologize. And if there's a scarlet woman here, I'll meet you in the bar in ten minutes.

Thank you for your indulgence. Without further delay I'll ask you to join me in a toast to my beautiful daughter, the bride, and her handsome hus-band, the groom. The bride and groom.

Father of the Bride — Example 2

The following speech was written, delivered by, and reproduced with the kind permission of Chris White.

This is a father of the bride speech that I doubt left many dry eyes in the house. It is very moving all the way through and even the comical lines have sentiment in them. The speech also contains a number of quotes, many of which you may want to make use of yourself.

To give the speech a witty and more personal tone, he includes an account of the groom asking permission to marry his daughter, perhaps slightly exaggerated, but that is all part of poetic license and adds to the humor of the speech.

Ladies and gentlemen, it is my very pleasant duty to welcome you here this evening to this special occasion of celebrating this marriage. I'm sure that you will all agree on how radiant and gorgeous the bride is. However, the groom is not too bad himself.

I know that some of you have traveled quite a distance to be with us here tonight, from both overseas and interstate. We really thank you and welcome you here tonight and hope that you really do enjoy yourselves accordingly. We are all very sad that the bride's grandfather is not here with us tonight. We all miss him, but I'm sure he is "watching down on us and is very proud and happy for her."

When they stood at the altar earlier today and she spoke those magic words "I do," I had cause to reflect that it's one of the few times in her life she's agreed to do something without question. Don't get me wrong, my daughter was wonderful and obedient as a child—with a bit of prompting.

As a child she was full of life, effervescence, fun and joy and was just so bubbly she made friends with everyone. During her teen years, both at school and at University, she had a wonderful time, being the first person to gain the distinction of getting her degree with no study at all. However she worked hard for her degree, and we congratulate her for it.

Then her Thespian Knight in Shining Armor in the form of the groom came along. I didn't doubt her choice at all, as Victor Hugo once said, "Men have sight, women have insight."

Now the groom is a very good actor, but with a somewhat "Puckish" sense of humor. At first we thought him a little shy, retiring and rather reluctant to talk with us, but we were victims of his talents. Beware! If you make the mistake of talking to the groom about himself or his exploits, have a friend ready to come and rescue you at a signal, otherwise you will find several hours gone, without you ever having to say a word. You will find him a real wordsmith, witty and with a quick, dry sense of humor.

The only time I have ever found the groom at a loss for words and without his sense of humor, suffering from severe stage fright—or should I say performance terror—was on a Sunday morning some time ago. (Why do these questions for my daughters' hands always get asked of me on Sunday mornings?) I was sitting in bed, reading the paper and quietly minding my own business, when I heard voices from downstairs. The next thing I saw was the groom ascending the stairs at a 60-degree tilt backward, white knuckles gripping the rails, with my daughter pushing him hard from behind.

He approached the end of the bed trembling and gripped it (I could feel it shaking and hear the metal rattling), and so by this time (not surprisingly) I had become quite interested in proceedings.

He finally blurted out that he and my daughter wanted to get married, and did they have my permission? I simply said, "Do you love her?" and he said, "Yes" and then I said, "Does she love you?" to which he replied, "Yes," and because I instantly recalled Benjamin Disraeli's comments on love: "We are all born for love. It is the principle of existence and its only end." I said "You have my blessing for this."

As you are both adults, I do not feel it my place to give advice, but as a father I now entrust my daughter to you safe in the knowledge that she is with a man who both loves and respects her just as much as she loves and respects you.

I am deeply grateful to you as the man who has given my little girl such joy, happiness, life and love, which she now radiates. A writer called Janos Arany once said: "In dreams and in love there are no impossibilities." That is my wish for you both. A marriage is a joining of two individuals. Although the bride and groom's lives are now symbolically one, it's important for each of you to realize that your partner is his or her own person.

As you come to understand and appreciate your differences, you will grow in trust, respect, and love—and then as you truly appreciate how much of this you have in common; your love will deepen even more. I can say this because I know that neither of you subscribe to the theory that "A wedding is like a funeral. There is the Service and then everyone cries... because your life is over." That was the piece of advice I said I was not going to give, but I did it anyway because this is my speech.

I am sure everyone here will agree what a beautiful bride she is, and the sight of them coming together as such a lovely couple makes the hard work and planning that has gone into this day worthwhile.

As I say this, I see that that my daughter has grown up, left home, and is now married. When I look back over the years, I realize how little time you really do have with your children. A philosopher once said: "Treasure the love you receive above all. It will survive long after your gold and good health have gone." We wish you all the happiness and prosperity in the world, and I am glad to welcome the groom and his family into our family.

In conclusion, I hope that none of you will go home thinking the words of Groucho Marks: "I've had a wonderful time, but this wasn't it." And so I would now ask you to raise your glasses and join me in a toast to the future health and happiness of the union of the bride and groom.

Father of the Bride – Example 3

The following speech was written, delivered by, and reproduced with the kind permission of Ian Taylor.

It is a reasonably short speech but it has all the right ingredients. A little bit of humor, a little bit of sentiment, and plenty of pride. It is self-deprecating but witty nonetheless and uses the speaker's own hobby, golf, as a source of amusement. Hobbies and interests can be a good source of inspiration to include in a speech, as a way of introducing humor or describing someone's personality. Here it is used as an opportunity to include a golfing joke, modified for the speaker's purposes.

Welcome, everyone. I believe, that as father of the bride, it is my dubious privilege to make the first speech, so, here's one I prepared earlier.

I would like to start by saying what a pleasure it is to welcome, on this very happy occasion all relatives and friends of both families. I'd like to take this opportunity to thank especially my wife for not only being tolerant but more importantly an outstanding mother and the guiding influence in the upbringing of our daughter, culminating in today's celebrations.

To the reverend (who unfortunately had to leave) our thanks for officiating at the ceremony, and to his "boss" for keeping the weather at bay.

Before I ask you to join me in a toast to the bride and groom, I'd like to bore you with a few words. I will try to keep them short, as I know that the other two speakers are really looking forward to standing here before you and making their speeches!

Nine months ago Nicola phoned and asked me what I was doing on Saturday, 23 March. As she knows that I *always* play golf on a Saturday, I thought she had taken up the game at long last and wanted to join me at Balmore Golf Club.

You must therefore realize that I'm here under duress as I had to give up my usual Saturday round of golf in order to be here today, but I wouldn't have missed it for the world. Talking of golf, I wonder if you've heard the story about the golfer who mis-hit a ball and as it bumbled along the fairway eventually reaching the green, his partner turned to him and said, "That's what I'd call a Sally Gunnell shot—runs like hell but not very pretty." I would like to describe the same shot in another way, "As a son-in-law shot—it turned out much better than we could ever have hoped for!"

We are very proud, to see our daughter, looking so radiant, on this her wedding day. During the time we've known the groom, we've come to realize how special he is to her and she is to him and we welcome him into our family. For those of you who don't know, she is our *only* daughter. She was a *perfect* daughter, well, she *is* a perfect daughter. What I'm really trying to say is that, as a child, she was *so perfect* a daughter we vowed *never* to have another.

Our daughter is very choosy when it comes to men, she has taken her time to find the love of her life … and it's no small feat what the groom has achieved, in winning her love.

A few months ago I asked my daughter what she was looking for in a marriage, and she said, "Love, happiness and companionship." Later, I asked the groom the same question, and after a little hesitation he eventually said, "I'd really like a new pool table!"

Apparently it's traditional for the bride's father to offer some worldly thoughts and advice about marriage. During the last twenty-seven years, I've learned a few things about it, so here goes:

> *[To the bride]* The definition of a perfect wife is one who helps her husband with the dishes.
> *[To the groom]*Remember, man is incomplete until he finds a wife—then he's finished!
> Never go to sleep with an unfinished argument hanging over you. Be a man! Stay awake and fight to the bitter end! You're going to lose anyway, so you might as well get it over and done with!

Proper Advice? Well, just keep four things in mind. The first is love, closely followed by friendship, then tolerance, and then communication. Easy to say, but they can be quite hard to carry out. You must both realize that marriage isn't easy, but it's not impossible. Many of us know that everyone faces ups and downs in a life commitment. There is no secret to a happy marriage. You'll both have to work at it, like many of us. There is no challenge in a marriage that cannot be overcome by the following three, three-word sentences. These are: I was wrong! You were right! I love you!

Here's to the past for all that you've learned. Here's to the present for all that you share. And here's to the future for all that you can look forward to together. Ladies and gentlemen, please be upstanding, and raise your glasses to the bride and groom. Thank you.

Father of the Bride—Example 4

The following speech was written, delivered by, and reproduced with the kind permission of Dave Everest.

It is a father of the bride speech with all the necessary ingredients: a little humor, a little sentiment, and a lot of love. It uses a visual prop (his mobile phone) at the beginning to open the speech and grab everyone's attention with a joke to break the ice. A few popular jokes are included in the rest of the speech, but what makes it unique is when he plays a song at the end before the toast.

[Stand up, mobile phone in hand] "Well thank you vicar it is a bit inconvenient at the moment I am just about to start the speeches."

I'm afraid there's been a bit of a hiccup in the proceedings; the vicar has just phoned to say that we have to do the registry signing all over again. It appears that the groom's pen wouldn't work so he borrowed the vicar's. He was still having problems so the vicar said, "Put your weight on it." *[To the bride]* I'm afraid that you are now Mrs. 179 lbs.

I'm only going to speak for a couple of minutes because of my throat, if I go on too long my wife has threatened to cut it. I've tried to memorize this speech, which isn't easy when you have the memory retention of a goldfish, so forgive me if I resort to my notes every five seconds.

When the happy couple announced that they were going to get married, I asked them what that entailed for me and my daughter said that I would have to give her away. To those of you who know me well, that came as a bit of a shock as I am not used to giving things away. Selling maybe, but giving away, I ask you. However, I did a deal with the groom, your tickets for a Wimbledon tennis match for my daughter. I hope you'll agree that he came out best.

My wife and I would like to welcome the groom's parents and all relatives and friends of both families to this very happy occasion. There are also several people who I wish could have been here but aren't and hopefully they are keeping an eye on proceedings from afar.

I would like to thank the beautiful bridesmaids for looking after the bride, the vicar for a lovely service, his boss for the great improvement in the weather and the staff at the hotel for the great food and service.

Clearly, large family events like today's don't just happen. They take a considerable amount of hard work and organization and it would seem an appropriate point, therefore, for me to ask you all to join me in a toast to my wife, as without her constant hard work and organizational skills, today would not have been the fine occasion that it is. To my wife. Any excuse for a drink.

It is I believe traditional to give an insight into the people whose marriage you have all just witnessed. My daughter has made a beautiful bride, but what sort of person is she? Well, for a start she isn't environmentally friendly. She wouldn't let us buy re-cycled toilet paper because she thought it was.

She has of course always brightened up our lives. You never did learn to turn lights off did you. She always complained that she had nothing to wear, but managed to fill six wardrobes and most of the floor with it. Funny that now she has her own house she is really house proud. Anyway she always dressed to kill, and cooked the same way. Only joking, we have had some lovely meals at your house.

She is a lovely girl and deserves a good husband. You're very lucky that she's married you, before she found one. Seriously though, the groom is a great guy and a real man. You come round to my house, turn on the sports channel and settle down, you even raid the fridge for *my* chocolate. You are also partially deaf which is a great male attribute.

By all accounts we are lucky that the groom is here today. I have it on good authority that when he was a baby, his mom went to the local shops and, as was the custom in those days, she left him outside in his smart pram. She bought the groceries and returned home. Sometime later, to her horror, she remembered that her baby was still outside the shop. Luckily he is here today none the worse for this experience!

I started planning this speech a month ago, and you must feel like I have been delivering it equally as long—so that is all from me.

No, I haven't quite finished. I am reminded of the wedding that we went to a few months ago where two of the guests were a minister and a priest. When the priest was offered a drink for the toast he said, " I'll have a large whiskey, please!" When the minister was offered the same, he said, "No thanks, I'd sooner go with a scarlet woman than touch the demon alcohol!" The priest promptly put his whiskey back on the tray, and said, "I didn't know there was a choice!"

Now I don't want to offend anybody, so if there's a priest or minister present, I apologize and if there's a scarlet woman here, I'll meet you in the bar after the speeches.

[Be very careful with this joke. It backfired on me. My sister-in-law, who I love dearly, was dressed all in scarlet!]

Anyway, I would like to finish off, by giving a few words of advice, to the newly weds. You must always consider the words of Oscar Wilde, "Women are meant to be loved, not understood."

Marriage will bring to you many things—loyalty, self restraint, obedience, a sense of fair play, and a whole host of other virtues that you wouldn't need had you remained single. Put the seat down after you. And remember those two invaluable words "Yes dear." And finally some musical advice. *[Play the first couple of verses of Bobby Vee's version of "Take Good Care of My Baby"]*

And now, at long last, I hear you say, it gives me great pleasure to propose the toast of long life and happiness to the bride and groom.

Brother of the Bride
—an alternative father of the bride speech

The following speech was written, delivered by, and reproduced with the kind permission of Yau Ming. The author and the speech come from Australia.

It is actually a "brother of the bride" speech and is performed in the sad absence of the bride's father. It is an excellent example of how a wedding speech can be good even without any humor. It is complimentary toward the bride and groom's families, demonstrates his affection for his sister without being too soppy, and provides all the necessary thanks to the relevant parties.

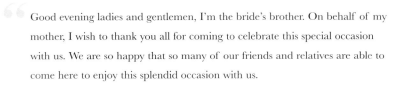

Good evening ladies and gentlemen, I'm the bride's brother. On behalf of my mother, I wish to thank you all for coming to celebrate this special occasion with us. We are so happy that so many of our friends and relatives are able to come here to enjoy this splendid occasion with us.

Today seems like a magical dream. This morning, I proudly walked my sister down the aisle to marry the man whom she loves so much. It was so beautiful to watch them exchanging their vows in that beautiful stained glass church. It's marvellous seeing these two good people come together. The Bride and Groom.

My daughter is a gem in our family, a blessing to both her parents and me. She's been a good and faithful daughter to my mom and my dad. We know she will also be a blessing to her husband and his family. Dad would be so proud to see you together with this man.

She has been a good sister to me. I will miss her wit and good company, especially when *South Park* is on. I'm sorry but the "higher authorities" will not allow me to do Cartman's German dance to honor this occasion.

My sister and I have been so close that we're almost telepathic. We used to simply exchange looks at each other to communicate jokes. But lately she's been a little distant. Her eyes like those of Skywalker look far far away.

[To the groom] I am so glad that you are marrying my sister. We have been good friends for a long time. He is a hardworking, talented, and ambitious young man. He not only has a good career path in I.T. but also a place in the *Guinness World Book of Records* as the holder of the biggest CD collection. But, above all these things, he loves my sister first and desires that she have the best. I know that my sister has found in you a partner, a trusted friend, a husband who will love her, honor her, cherish, and take good care of her.*[Face audience]*

I believe this because when he was courting my sister, he honored my family, my sister, and his God by being patient like Jacob. He waited for the right and appropriate time to ask for my sister's hand in marriage last year.

If my father were alive today he would be proud to give his daughter's hand in marriage to you. Instead, today I have that honor.

[To the groom's parents] I am so happy that my sister is marrying into such a good hearted family. I could not have asked for better in-laws; you both are the most kind, warm, and friendly people I've known. I know you will take only the best care of my sister.

[Thanks ushers, helpers and pastor]

Today, we are surrounded by so many friends and family members who have been important to us. Some have traveled hundreds of miles, just to be here today.

Would you all please rise and join me—in this first of many toasts—to wish the bride and groom a long and happy married life together.

May your lives be entwined like the strong leaves of ivy on a high castle tower. May your joy never end like the circles of your wedding rings.

Sister of the Bride
–an alternative father of the bride speech

The following speech was written, delivered by, and reproduced with the kind permission of Rebecca Hemnant.

This is more or less an equivalent of a father of the bride speech as it was delivered after "giving the bride away." This example shows that a well written speech can be delivered by either a male or female, whatever role they are playing in the wedding. The speaker describes the bride's personality well and gives the audience a good picture, through her childhood remembrances, of their close relationship.

For those of you that don't already know me I'm the bride's "slightly" older sister. When she first asked me to give her away I felt two things, the first was one of extreme and enormous pride that she'd asked me, and the second was "Oh my God" I have to do a speech. But please don't worry, this won't take too long.

I would like to thank the vicar for a lovely service, the vicar's mate for keeping an eye out on the weather, and the beautiful bridesmaid. I am also delighted to have my mom, sisters, and brother here today to celebrate this day, one which I hope is the start of many more "happiest days of their life."

My sister has given me, and all of my family some incredibly happy and joyous moments over the years. She was a delight to grow up with, and has always provided us with some memorable moments. Having known her all her life I have a huge library of stories to leave her embarrassed and humiliated, but out of respect for her on her big day I have decided *not* to tell them.

So I'm not going to tell you about the milkman, yes they were around in those days, asking me how my brother was on many an occasion— well done mum, my sister always loved that hair cut.

And I'm not going to admit that I did my bit toward her hairstyles when I cut her fringe to about ½ inch and it took most of the next five years to grow back. In fact I'm surprised she ever forgave me! I can so clearly remember the horror on her face when I finally let her see it.

The bride, as I'm sure you all know is fiercely independent—I am reminded of a particular suitcase, a small red one, that was often packed on her way to leave home for one shore or another, and this one's first outing was to go back to Yorkshire with my uncle, even then an old man, when she was about four years old. As far as I can recall the only things she'd actually packed were books.

When she first introduced the groom to us all, well we weren't quite sure what to make of him really, and I'm sure he felt exactly the same. I think someone coming into a family of four sisters and a brother can find the whole experience quite daunting but he took it all in his stride and has since become the comedian and magician of family social events.

On a more serious note, I hope you all agree that the wedding so far, has been a huge success, I would like to thank all of you for celebrating the day with us, especially those who have traveled almost the length of the country to be here.

It has been an absolute honor for me, to give you away today; you are a fantastic sister, great daughter, and brilliant friend. I've never seen you happier than you have been over these last few years with the groom; I hope the best for you now and always.

Finally, on behalf of my mom, my sisters, and brother, and of course all our partners, I would like to welcome the groom, his mom and dad into our family. We all look forward to getting to know you better.

Now, ladies and gentleman, it gives me great pleasure to invite you all to stand and raise your glasses in a toast to the bride and groom. To love, laughter, and happily ever after. Cheers!

Groom Speeches

While the groom's speech isn't necessarily expected to be humorous, most of the speeches in this section do contain a certain amount of jokes or funny lines. Some of the speeches are very short and simply express the feelings of the groom (and his wife). It is often a balancing act, trying to strike the right chord by offering humor and entertainment for the audience as well as expressing more serious feelings. It is also a choice for the speaker whether they feel confident enough to deliver a long speech with funny lines or whether to keep it short and sweet and use it as a way of offering thanks. The main things to include in a groom's speech are:

* Thanking your new father-in-law for his speech and for his beautiful daughter.
* Thanking the guests for sharing your day and for their gifts.
* Thanking both sets of parents for their help with your wedding.
* Giving a small gift to the two mothers.
* Complimenting your new wife.
* Thanking the best man for his help and giving gifts to

      him and the rest of the bridal party.

   * Offering a toast to the bridesmaids.

The giving of gifts is optional, but the main purpose of the speech is to offer thanks on behalf of the bride and groom to attendants and those who have helped organize, or contribute toward it.

Groom Speech–Example 1

The following speech was written, delivered by, and reproduced with the kind permission of Martin Carter. It contains an example of everything to include when speaking as a groom at your wedding reception. It is humorous but in no way offensive, and moving without being soppy.

He makes reference to the research he's done on the Internet and uses this as a well-timed joke to introduce the fact that he has two best men. Using statistics (or spoof statistics) can be a good source of humor and a way of developing a speech.

"Ladies and gentlemen, you are about to witness a unique event in history—the very first and last time that my wife is going to let me speak on behalf of both of us. It is a privilege and an honor to do so. I just hope that, so soon into our married life, I don't let her down.

Today has so far been a day beyond my wildest dreams. As a child, dreaming of my wedding day, I never dared imagine that I would end up marrying someone so intelligent, so witty, so popular, so gorgeous, and so altogether fantastic…*[To his wife]* Is this O.K. so far?

Ladies and gentlemen, it is apparently my job to do all the thankyous. The first and biggest thankyou is to all of you. Thank you all for choosing to share today with us. We are delighted and touched to see so many of you here. And thank you, of course, for all the wonderful gifts.

The father of the bride, on the other hand, who is picking up the bill for dinner, is completely distraught. When he saw the guest list with addresses in Ireland, Egypt, the U.S.A., Scotland, as well as the four corners of England, he was delighted, since he felt sure that most of you wouldn't make the effort to turn up. It's to his credit that during his speech you would never have guessed he is in fact a broke, or rather a broken, man.

On the subject of his speech I'd like to thank him for his kind words. I hope that, as his daughter's husband, I can live up to the image he painted of me or, failing that, at least continue to keep pulling the wool over his eyes!

We would also like to thank my wife's parents for all their efforts in organizing today. Their support has been invaluable, advice sound, and checkbook largely available. I'd personally like to thank them for making me feel so welcome right from the very second time I met them. I feel immensely fortunate to have married into such a great family. My sincere wish is that together we can build a home that is as welcoming and as full of love and happiness as theirs is (personally speaking I also quite like the idea of five bedrooms, three bathrooms, and a big garden too).

Of course, my wife is just one of three wonderful sisters but on the basis that the best things come in small packages, I believe I have landed the pick of the bunch. She loves her sisters dearly and really appreciates the help and support which they have given her, not just as her bridesmaids today, but throughout her life. I would say they've been a shoulder to cry on but frankly she has never been able to reach that high. Nonetheless, thank you anyway on behalf of my wife for all your love and support down the years and for making me feel so welcome.

Of course the other young lady who played a big part today is our flower girl, who I'm sure you will all agree not only looked absolutely gorgeous, but also did a great job of handing out the roses at the church. You probably noticed that the roses, which she was giving out at church, were bought on behalf of the British Heart Foundation. This is a charity very close to our hearts—excuse the pun—because my dad had heart surgery sixteen years ago. In fact it was when I was going through my teenager years, although I'm sure that's just coincidence. It is thanks to the work of charities like the B.H.F. that my dad is here today. I can't even begin to tell you just how much it means to me that he is here… and not just because he's paying for the booze.

Mom and dad, thanks for everything that you have given me during my life and for all your help in planning today—we couldn't have done it without you. Thanks for bringing me up the way you have, for all of your encouragement and support. But most of all thank you for instilling in me whatever it is that convinced my wife that she wanted to marry me; on that score alone, I think you can be justifiably proud of yourselves; I am certainly proud to have you as my parents.

There are just a few more people I need to thank. First the two guys sitting at the end of the table, who despite their appearance aren't bouncers but are in fact my best men. While I was preparing this speech, I came across a website that had a series of questions for brides on it. One in particular caught my eye. The question was "If your groom didn't turn up would you, as tradition dictates, marry the best man?" According to the results, eighty percent said no, twelve percent of the brides said yes, and eight percent had said, given half a chance they'd have married the best man in the first place. Well, at least I gave my wife plenty of choice and what an enviable—or do I mean unenviable—choice it would have been?

So, I've got two best men. And they have indeed lived up to that billing. When I told people who I had picked there were a few raised eyebrows, as neither of them are particularly renowned for their organization, planning, or timekeeping skills. But in the end my confidence was well placed. The boys have done me proud and have both risen to the occasion, which is, I'm told, a rare and generally unexpected achievement for either of them these days. Guys, thanks very much for all your help and for organizing a great stag do, which I'm told I enjoyed enormously.

I should perhaps just mention at this point that they suffer from a rare medical condition which makes them prone to embellishment. They often invent the most fanciful stories, which they sincerely believe to be true. I hope that you will all bear this in mind when they stand up to speak in a few moments.

And so to my penultimate thankyou; to our ushers and very good friends, without whom today might well not have happened, because it was through them that we met at university, very nearly a decade ago.

For anyone who knew our university, it will come as no surprise to hear that we first met in "The Pav"—the student union. For anyone who knew my wife at university, it will also come as no surprise to hear that, at the time, she was standing at the bar. It was, in fact her very first night at university. Well, they do say, start as you mean to go on. She, however, can't remember meeting me. Obviously the excitement and anticipation of being at university made that whole first evening in the bar a bit of a blur. I'm sure it also explains why she was slurring her words and swaying from side to side slightly as she spoke. So it took me a few weeks to catch her eye but, when we did eventually get it together, there were fireworks…it was November 5, 1992.

Nearly ten years might sound like a long time between first date and wedding day. But that is not because we have been reluctant to make a commitment. It's just that we never quite managed to stay still for long enough. With the exception of Manchester in 1992 and London now, we have always lived a long way from each other, clocking up fifteen cities or countries between us. Much of our relationship has been spent on planes, trains, and in cars. Surely it has to be more than a coincidence that since we've lived in the same city, British Airways' profits have plummeted, Railtrack has gone into administration, and the oil price has crashed?

But the truth is, is that, even when we have been a long way apart, I have felt that a part of her has always gone with me. And that's why asking her to marry me, while being the biggest commitment I have ever made, was also the easiest, because above all else, she is my soul mate and my best friend.

So you'll be glad to hear that I've come to my final thankyou. Thank you for marrying me. I am devoted to you, I have so much to thank you for, and I love you with all of my heart. You look absolutely stunning today, but then, you look stunning to me every day. It's been a long road, but we got there in the end and I know that whatever the future holds we'll live it happily together.

Of course this doesn't explain *why* it has taken us so long to get married. Well, outside church today, I was talking to one of her friends and she told me that, according to my wife, its all about maturity. She had asked my wife why we were getting married now, after all this time, and her response was this…

"Men are like a fine wine. They all start out as grapes. It's our job to stamp on them and then keep them in the dark until they mature into something you'd like to have dinner with…"

It is my eternal good fortune that my wife's taste in wine is cheap, unrefined, and immature.

Ladies and Gentlemen, thank you again for being here today, for the wonderful gifts, for your good wishes and most of all for your friendship now and in the future. Here's to a wonderful evening.

Groom Speech–Example 2

The following speech was written, delivered by, and reproduced with the kind permission of Gregory Prasad. It was performed at a wedding in the U.S.A. in August 2002 and while it contains some excellent lines of humor, the most interesting part of this speech is the final few paragraphs where the author talks about his new bride.

One thing to bear in mind if you intend on using a similar sentimental section in your own speech is that weddings are very emotional, especially for the bride and groom. When it comes to the actual reading of the speech you may find that the tears are not just visible in the members of the audience, they may also be seen in the eyes of the reader.

" I was going to begin with "ladies and gentlemen" but on looking around I'm glad I didn't. So here goes.

Distinguished guests, those of lesser distinction, and those of no distinction at all, family, relatives, new and old, in-laws and out-laws, friends, friends of friends, and freeloaders, welcome to our wedding reception.

First of all I would like to thank my brothers and my new sister for their kind words.

I did have a speech all worked out for this special occasion, but of course now that I'm a married man, she has told me what to say instead. So here goes:

On behalf of my wife—and I suppose I'm going to have to get used to saying that—I would like to start by thanking everyone here today for sharing our very special day with us. A lot of people have traveled far to be here tonight and we are delighted to see you all. Thank you for your cards, kind thoughts, wedding gifts, and especially the big checks! And, of course, all these smiling faces I see in front of me tonight. I hope you can all get the opportunity to mingle tonight, get to know each other a little better, and, naturally, have a good time.

I would like to take this opportunity to thank my parents for my upbringing and the sacrifices they have made for me. I would like to thank them both for the advice they have given me, for putting up with me, and for pointing me in the right direction—usually only to watch me go off and do exactly the opposite, of course—but that's what sons are for and do best.

To my new mom and dad, I would like to thank you so much for everything you have done and for welcoming me so openly into your family. I feel very proud to be able to say that I am your son-in-law and will always do my best to live up to your expectations and promise to take care of your daughter—and of course do everything she tells me to do—now I'm not saying she's bossy, but you know just as well as I do…

This whole day, and everything else you have given us, has been so overwhelming. We never expected all of this and you have both made us feel very special. I'm sure everyone will agree what a fantastic display it has been so far.

I would like to thank you most importantly for giving me your blessing to marry your beautiful and intelligent daughter. I hope that you don't feel that you've lost a daughter, but that you have gained another mouth to feed and someone to clean up after. [*Pause.*] By the way dad, I have not forgotten. I'll sign the receipt for you. Dad has written out a receipt for me.

It says: Received one daughter in perfect condition, fully guaranteed, fully warranted. Comes complete with extras. Keep topped up with expensive jewelry, and lubricate well with fine wines. Service regularly with lavish trips to exotic and faraway places.

Warning: has a tendency to get irritable if doesn't have the final say on *everything*. Thanks, I'll keep that in mind. Care notes: gets bored easily, keep busy with a constant supply of chores. Hey, I could do that!

Not to be outdone, my dad has written out a receipt for my wife as well. It reads:

Received one son, sold as seen, no refunds under any circumstances. We've redecorated the room and changed the locks, so you're stuck with him.

Care notes: dehydrates easily, top up regularly with beer and any other alcoholic beverages.

This brings me on to the best man. Well…the best I could get at short notice. Twenty-four years of pain and misery he has caused me. Earlier today he handed me a whole script to say all these kind and wonderful comments that I should tell you about him. Unfortunately, all this did was reinstate my belief of the fact that he is a compulsive liar and anything that he tells you should not be believed for one moment. Seriously, I could not think of anyone I would rather be my best man for the wedding…I tried…but they were all booked with other plans. Thanks for all your help.

The maid of honor, I have known for quite some time. Although we have never always seen eye to eye on everything, we are still really good friends. And now she is officially my new little sister. I have never had a little sister before, so now I get to abuse someone in a whole new fashion. You are a fantastic cook and it looks like every holiday we are going to spend at your house. But really, thank you for your support and help in making this such a wonderful day.

To the rest of the bridal party, thank you as well for your assistance.

Now that I have finished one half here goes the other,

[Thanks groom's party], the list goes on, thank you all for making this day very special to us.

It is said that "you don't marry someone you can live with—you marry the person who you cannot live without," which is very true with my wife. While looking forward and preparing myself for today I wasn't prepared enough for when I saw her walk down the stairs shining with sheer elegance and grace. I was overwhelmed to the say the least by how beautiful she looked this afternoon. I should be used to it now as she always dresses to kill, and unfortunately cooks the same way too. Although I shouldn't complain about her cooking, she prepared a lovely meal a few days ago, only slightly burning it, but it was still a lovely salad.

I want everyone here, especially my wife, to know how lucky I feel to be here right now. My wife is beautiful, intelligent, hardworking, caring. The list of her good qualities is extremely long. But, unfortunately I can't seem to read her handwriting...

But seriously, to my wife, my best friend and the love of my life, thank you for everything you have done. You know everything about me, including the really bad stuff, and love me just the same. I have my faults, yet you still agreed to marry me. I am extremely lucky today to be the one to marry you and I know this is the start of many happy years together.

You have stood by me through a lot of decisions since we got together. You agreed to make me the happiest man in the world today and have a natural way that makes every day a joy to be with you. I know that I told you earlier but I want everyone to know how beautiful you look today. Your dress is stunning and you really do look like a little princess. You have made me the happiest and proudest man alive today by saying "I do" and I can't wait to tell everyone that you are my wife at every opportunity I have. I don't have to hope that our future together will be a happy one, I know it will be, because every day I wake to find that I love you twice as much as the day before. As my wife will tell you—I'm sometimes wrong, but in marrying, I know I've made the right decision. Thank you darling.

Thank you all for joining us tonight. We know we are surrounded by loved ones. Please enjoy the rest of the night and have a great time.

Groom Speech – Example 3

The following speech was written, delivered by, and reproduced with the kind permission of John Baird. You will see that the speech contains a couple of very similar, if not exactly the same, jokes, and gags that also appeared in the previous speech. The two are shown together to illustrate how the same type of jokes can be used in very different speeches.

This speech flows very well and while it doesn't contain quite as much sentiment as the last one, it does contain the main ingredients that are needed to produce an excellent groom's speech.

Thank you for your kind words, I am very proud to be your son-in-law; I hope I can live up to your expectations. I would sincerely like to thank you for welcoming me into your family, for bringing up such a lovely daughter, and for giving me your blessing to marry her.

In addition, due to the number of phone calls between my wife and her mom, the phone company would also like to thank you both.

On this date in history in 1889 the Boer War ended, and maybe after my speech you'll think it's started again, although this day will go down in history as the day you all heard the best ever speech. It will be read shortly by one of my best men.

It is said that a great speech has a good beginning, a good ending, and most importantly, the two are as close together as possible.

[Have a thick wad of paper to hand]

Well tough!

[Unfold notes, pause, and smile at all tables]

That, of course, was a cracker of a speech of my own worked out for you today, but as I am now married, my wife has handed this to me to say instead. *[To the father-in-law]* By the way, I haven't forgotten, I'll sign that receipt for you: *[Produce bit of paper with the writing on saying]*

Received, one daughter in perfect condition, fully guaranteed. Care notes: gets bored easily, keep busy with constant supply of chores. Comes complete with all extras. (My favorite's the nurse's uniform.)

Not to be outdone though my dad also has a receipt for my wife to sign. It reads: *[Again, pull out another bit of paper]*

Received, one son, sold as seen, no refunds under any circumstances. We've redecorated the room and changed the locks so you're stuck with him. Care Notes: dehydrates easily, top up regularly with beer.

I would now personally like to thank my best men. I have been best man to both of them and now it's my turn to go from the witness box to the dock—I bet my wife brings that up for the next fifty years. They have been a tower of strength throughout the proceedings, as through my life, and what better way to reward them as to let them get me back for the speeches I did at their weddings. I'd like to give these to you. *[Hand gifts to them]*

On behalf of my wife and I, we would like to thank the rest of you for your "presence" in both senses of the word, and for sharing our special day with us. Especially those who have traveled from far away places like Holland, Ireland, Margate, and the north of England to be here. We are very grateful, although it never surprises me how far some people would go for a free meal.

We have been planning this wedding for about a year now, although it seems like a lifetime. Well, I say "we," my wife did all the work, I just agreed to sort out the weather. *[If hot add: and might I say a good job has been done. It wasn't easy but nevertheless I made it hot today. If cold add: And I even got that wrong.]*

I met my wife at Eros nightclub and I should say thanks to my friend over there *[point to friend]* for introducing me. They say: "You don't marry someone you can live with, you marry the person who you cannot live without," which is very true with my wife and, while looking forward and preparing myself for today, I wasn't prepared enough for when I saw her walk down the aisle radiating elegance and grace. I was overwhelmed, to the say the least, by how beautiful she looked.

I should be used to it now as she always dresses to kill, unfortunately she cooks the same way. Although I shouldn't have a go at her cooking that much. She made a lovely meal a few days ago only slightly burning it, but it was a lovely salad. Only kidding.

I'd like to propose a toast:

To my bride: she knows all about me and loves me just the same.

Today also represents a great occasion for both my parents who, as well as putting up with me and pointing me in the right direction, have prepared me well, supported me through my life and taught me the difference between right and wrong, so as that I know which I am enjoying at any given time!

A final and big thankyou goes to our bridesmaids who looked lovely and I thank them all for doing such a wonderful job today. *[Gives them gifts]*

[Toast bridesmaids]

Ladies and Gentlemen, please stand. I would like to propose a toast to the bridesmaids.

Well, I could stand here and give you a load more stale old jokes, but instead I think I'll leave that to one of my best men who has cut his speech by quite a lot so as not to be Tottenham's first case of foot in mouth disease, just remember he's never been one to let the truth get in the way of a good story. Ladies and gentlemen, my best man.

Groom Speech – Example 4

The following speech was written, delivered by, and reproduced with the kind permission of Rob Cargill. The speech is fairly short in length, however the author has managed to include all the necessary parts to ensure the speech would be well received. Reading through the speech, you will see that the groom has used the wedding date as a source for funny lines, comparing their marriage with celebrity couples for comic effect. The reference to Madonna's music is particularly funny.

While preparing this speech I thought it would be interesting to see if any celebrity couples had been married on the same day as us. Paul Simon and Carrie Fisher wed in 1983…and split up after 9 months. Oh dear.

Also, Madonna married Sean Penn on this day in 1985; and we all know the outcome of that.

Unlike the latter, while Lisa is "Like A Virgin," I plan to "Cherish" her forever, and I am not afraid to "Justify My Love." There's always the "Hanky Panky" to look forward to. There are children present, so the less said about "Get into the Groove" the better.

We have been together for nearly ten years, and it's been the happiest decade of my life. We first got together at a Halloween party, where she was dressed up as a witch's cat and I was dressed as a crazy axe murderer. I was instantly smitten with that kitten I can tell you.

She stuck with me through my scabby student days, and she's even managed to suffer living with me for five years. At home, we're the perfect team—I mess up the house and she tidies. I affectionately call her my Mrs. Mop.

In 1998 I popped the question, so like Elvis's toilet door twenty-five years ago, we've been engaged for a long time. Today she's made me the happiest man on earth, she's my bride and joy. And I think you'll all agree she's done a superb job organizing today almost single-handed.

[Toasts]

Please join me and raise a glass to my beautiful bride. To the bride!

We'd like to thank the bridesmaids for all their help in the preparation for today, and I think you'll agree they look fantastic. We have some gifts for you. *[Hand gifts to them and toasts]*

To the bridesmaids.

We'd like to say a big thank you to our moms for all their love and support over the years. You've both been really good to us. So please join us in a toast. To the moms.

Big thanks to the best man, my dear brother. I'm not sure I should give you the gift now with your speech pending. This man had the easiest job on the day, or perhaps he just made it look easy. For someone who's not too steady on his legs (you should have seen him in Amsterdam), he made walking up the aisle an art form today. Thanks for all your help over the years bro'. To the best man.

For being there when we needed him, my dad has always helped us out. Boney M had him in mind when they wrote "Daddycool." Please raise your glasses and drink a toast. To my dad.

And last but not least, we come to the ushers. I've known these chaps for years and they have certainly done the business today. Let's raise our glasses one more time please. To the ushers.

And now for the bit you've all been waiting for, the best man's speech. I don't mind admitting I'm scared, please be kind. Over to you bruv.

Groom Speech–Example 5

The following speech was written, delivered by, and reproduced with the kind permission of Trevor Morgan. It is another reasonably short speech and you will see that it once again contains the receipt gag. I should mention that even though the same gag appears in three of the first five example speeches, most of your wedding guests will not have heard it. How many weddings does the average person go to?

It is apparent from the opening few lines of this speech that the groom has an excellent relationship with the bride's parents and this can be really useful, not just in the future, for obvious reasons, but it can also make the speech more humorous. This speech is also a good example of using events in history that happened on the same date as a source of humor.

Thank you for those lovely words. I'd like to remind you that you're not so much losing a daughter, but regaining three wardrobes.

I shan't forget the first time my wife took me home to meet her parents. To break the ice, I asked her dad which football team he supported. "West Ham" he replied. Which was obvious as he lives in London. So I said "I bet it's exciting when you win a match." "I don't know," he replied, "I've only been supporting them for six seasons."

By the way, I haven't forgotten, I'll sign that receipt for you. He has written out a receipt for me. It reads: Received: one daughter in perfect condition, fully guaranteed. Care Notes: gets bored easily, keep busy with a constant supply of chores.

Not to be outdone, my mom also has a receipt for my wife to sign. It reads: Received: one son, sold as seen, no refunds under any circumstances. I've re-decorated the room and changed the locks so you're stuck with him. Care Notes: de-hydrates easily, top up regularly with beer.

While writing this speech, I thought it would be a good idea to research some events in history which happened on this day. I found out that on this day in 1889 Sherlock Holmes appeared in the *Adventure of The Engineer's Thumb* and in 1948 synthetic rubber was first used in asphaltic concrete. I'm sure both of these events will be a real inspiration to us over the years.

Now, there are some thankyous that I'd like to convey on behalf of my wife and I. We both want to thank the bride's parents for the support they've given us. From day one, you have been fully behind us, and have always demonstrated how a marriage should be—and that's successful. I'll do my best to live up to your expectations and promise to take good care of your daughter. And, of course, do everything that she tells me to do.

Mother-in-law—I am very happy to be able to call myself your son-in-law, and I'm also looking forward to being able to tell mother-in-law jokes in the future. Now, I wouldn't say my mother-in-law's cooking is bad, but when we go round for dinner, we pray after we eat.

Mom, I want to say a special thank you to you. You've given me so much love and support over the years, have always been there for me when

I've needed you, and have been given a wonderful start in life. Thank you also for all the guidance and advice you've given me, for putting up with me and for pointing me in the right direction—usually only to watch me go off and do exactly the opposite—but of course, that's what sons are for and do best of all. I am very fortunate and proud that you are my mom.

We would also like to thank you all for your "presence," in both senses of the word. But most of all, it's especially warming to see all the smiling faces in front of us, some of whom have come from a long way. We would also like to remember those people who couldn't be here in person. But I know they are here in our hearts, minds, and souls.

Thank you to all of those involved in the wedding arrangements including the toastmaster, the guitarist, and the staff here, all of whom have helped make the day for us.

Especially, we'd like to thank my mom, my wife's mom and dad, the best man, and the bridesmaids. As a small token of our gratitude, we have some gifts to give out.

My biggest thank you is to my wife.

I want to thank you for being here now, even though you're probably suffering in silence. For those that don't know, she put her back out last week, and has been in agony since. It has nothing to do with me I might add. Today, your outfit looks fantastic, and you look stunning in it. Although I must admit though that when I saw the color of your dress, I was a bit disappointed, as it means the dishwasher doesn't match the fridge anymore—never mind.

We have known each other as friends for around ten years, but didn't start dating each other until four years ago. It was after work on an August summer evening, I was in the pub with my friend, Miss Stella Artois, and I noticed her on another table. I thought I'd play hard to get, and so totally ignored her. But as the night went on, my friend got more and more insistent that I talk to her. Eventually, I had no choice so I staggered over, thrust a drink in her hand, and we have never looked back. Not the most romantic way to ask her out, but certainly the most effective. I am very proud to be your husband, and I couldn't have asked for a better person to share the rest of my life with.

Finally, thank you once again to our bridesmaids today. So would everyone please join me in a toast to the two beautiful bridesmaids. Now, please suspend your belief for the next five minutes, as you listen to the best man's speech.

$G\,r\,o\,o\,m$ $S\,p\,e\,e\,c\,h-\mathcal{E}\,x\,a\,m\,p\,l\,e$ 6

The following speech was written, delivered by, and reproduced with the kind permission of Sanjay Jhangiani.

Once again, while it's not a long speech, it does contain all the important points of a groom's speech. The first few paragraphs are, as far as I know, quite unique and a good ice breaker. They include reference to some statistics that the groom came across; whether real of imaginary these are a great way of adding humor to the speech.

Ladies and gentleman, I have to be honest with you all and admit that I am quite nervous about standing up here and speaking this evening.

While I was writing my speech I came across some interesting facts about what guests are thinking about during a wedding speech. Apparently, twenty percent of you are thinking about getting onto the dance floor and partying the night away. Thirty percent of you are thinking about the marital status of the best man. Ladies, you may be pleased to know that he is single. He's also not very fussy as he showed on the stag do. It turns out that twenty percent of you are thinking about what happened on the stag do. Moving swiftly on. Ten percent of you are thinking about the type of couple that we will make. But rather worryingly from my point of view it turns out that fifteen percent of you are having romantic thoughts about the person sitting next to you.

There are several people here tonight who I would like to thank.

I'd like to start by thanking my parents for everything they have done in raising me. They have loved and supported me through every stage of my life and I am so grateful to them for all the advice they have given me and for always pointing me in the right direction. I'd also like to thank them for all the hard work and effort they have put in to make this day a success.

I would like to thank my wife's parents for the kindness that they have shown me and for welcoming me into their family. I'd also like to thank them for bringing up such a beautiful and intelligent daughter. I'll leave you to argue over which trait comes from whom.

Thank you to my wonderful sister for being such a great friend. I am very grateful for all the advice and the support. However, I must say one thing—I just cannot wait to do my speech when you get married I will get my revenge. I'd also just like to take this opportunity to wish you a happy birthday.

Thank you to my best man. I am very grateful for all the hard work and effort that you have put in over the last few weeks. I've known you for ten years now, and despite my concerns regarding what you would plan for my stag do and your speech, you have been, and will continue to be, a great friend. And so that brings me to my wife—my best friend. She is beautiful, she is intelligent, she is hard working, she is… what does that say? I'm having a little difficulty reading your handwriting. No, but on a more serious note, thank you for marrying me and making me the happiest man in the world. I am often wrong, but in marrying her, I know I have made the right decision.

Finally, I would like to thank all of you for attending and sharing this special day with us. Many of you have traveled hundreds of miles to be here and having you all here has helped to make this the most memorable and happy day of our lives.

All that's left for me to say is please all enjoy the rest of the night and have a great time.

Groom Speech — Example 7

The following speech was written, delivered by, and reproduced with the kind permission of David Mais. It is a very straightforward speech with all the necessary thanks and compliments that a groom would need to offer.

I've put a bit of a speech together today, but after the previous speaker sent us all to sleep I'll try to make mine a bit more interesting and entertaining. Sorry, only joking.

Before I start with my thankyous, have you all seen the "fun cameras" on your tables? Please feel free to take photos throughout the day. I think it'll be a good idea to take them early on as I don't expect many people will be able to focus very well as the day progresses and the drink starts to flow.

So, on behalf of my beautiful wife and I, we would like to thank you all for coming along, and sharing this very special day with us. And a huge thankyou for the wonderful presents.

I would like everybody here, especially my wife, to know how lucky and proud I am to be standing here today speaking to you as her husband. She is beautiful, caring, intelligent, charming and *[pause]*… What's that?… I can't read your writing darling!

Seriously though, I am overwhelmed at how beautiful she looks, and can't believe how privileged I am that she has become my wife. I am amazed to see her smiling and enjoying herself as she has been so stressed organizing what you will all agree has so far been a wonderful day. She has organized today's events almost single handedly.

I would like to propose a toast to the ushers and bridesmaids who I think you will agree with me look almost as beautiful as my wife—the brides-maids that is, not the ushers, they just look like… ushers—for the wonderful job they have done today and I'd like them to receive a small gift as a token of our appreciation.

I'd also like to thank *[the bride's parents]* for the help you've given us both emotionally and financially. We have a small gift for you as a token of our appreciation. I have to thank you for bringing up such a beautiful and intelligent daughter. I'll leave you to argue over which trait comes from whom.

They are the best father and mother-in-law anyone could wish for and I appreciate everything they have done for me in the last six years and I love them to bits. I'd like to thank my friend for arranging the mini bus at short notice when the limo didn't turn up and making it possible for us all to go to my stag do. What a great weekend we had, we won't forget that for a long time. I'd also like to thank everyone who came with me for what was a brilliant weekend.

Hope you all appreciate the lovely cake before us. I woke up last Sunday morning thinking I was going to London to pick up the cake but it turned out the cake was the other side of Leeds. So I'd like to thank my friend for traveling up to Harrogate to fetch it.

On a final note (who said thank god!) I'd just like to say how much we've been looking forward to today but more importantly we want everyone to enjoy the day as much as we are.

So now my thanks to my best man. I know you're waiting for his wonderful speech, so I'll now pass you over to him. No pressure mate.

Thanks everyone. *[Little bow]*

Groom Speech – Example 8

The following speech was written, delivered by, and reproduced with the kind permission of Darren Lord. This final groom's speech is much longer than the other examples that we have shown. In it the groom describes when he first met his wife, refers to his son, and describes the best man, as well as the usual thanks and compliments to his new wife.

Ladies and gentlemen: I would like to thank the previous speaker for those sincere words and to the bride's parents for the love that they have both shown me, not only in preparation for today, but from the first moment that we met some two and a half years ago.

I don't know who was more surprised that first night when my future wife brought me home without warning, when they were sitting there all ready for bed in their satin bath robes and her dad in his Snoopy slippers.

Anyway, quickly moving on... I did have a speech all worked out for this occasion, but of course now that I'm a married man, my wife has insisted that I read from the one that she has written for me.

So here goes: On behalf of my wife and I—I suppose I'm going to have to get used to saying that—I would like to start by thanking everyone here today for sharing our very special day with us. Thank you for all the wonderful gifts and cards that you have given us, we are very touched at your generosity.

We have both been very nervous about today and it means a great deal to us that you are sharing our day with us, and we hope that you are enjoying the occasion every bit as much as we are.

Most people on their wedding day describe it as the happiest day of their lives. That worries me, because it implies that as from tomorrow there's a lifelong decline ahead, so I'm making the most of today. However, I'm so happy today that even days less happy would still be blissful.

I would like to say a special thank you to those of you that have traveled some distance to be here today. It is quite a humbling experience to realize that you have friends and family that care so much for you. And I do genuinely mean that.

[To the bride's parents] I would like to thank you so much for everything you have done and for welcoming me so openly into your family.

I feel very proud to be able to say that I am your son-in-law and will always do my best to live up to your expectations, and promise to take care of your daughter—and of course do everything she tells me to do. Now I'm not saying she's bossy, but I know my place.

The whole day and everything else you have given us has been so overwhelming. We never expected all of this and you have both made us feel very special. I'm sure everyone will agree what a fantastic day it has been so far—even the weather has been on our side.

And, most importantly, thank you for giving me your blessing to marry your beautiful and intelligent daughter. I hope that you don't feel that you've lost a daughter, but have gained another mouth to feed and someone to clean up after.

I also want to say a special thankyou to my mom. Mom, you have been there for me constantly. To have brought us up on your own as you did in our younger days with so much love, care, and guidance has made you not only an amazing person but also my best friend. I am very fortunate and proud to have you as my mom. During my teenage years, *[mom's partner]* you gave my mom everything she deserved and became an amazing father figure.

I would like to thank you both for the advice you have given me, for putting up with me and for pointing me in the right direction. And for welcoming my wife into the family with open arms and supporting her as much as you do. Mom, don't worry I will still come round to see you—and, at the same time, get you to cook a meal, wash my laundry, and generally leave a mess behind—so nothing really changes!

[Groom's family] you have been a huge help with the house. I am not sure we could have done it without you. You know that we owe you so much for the support and help when we moved in. I just hope that in the happiness of our marriage we can repay some of what you have done for us. It is at this point that I would like to give some flowers to both our moms, for being two very inspirational figures in our life. And may I just add that you both look beautiful today. *[Present flowers]*

As some of you know there is an age gap between my wife and I—although as a gentleman I will not tell you exactly how much younger I am. For our first official date—I say the first official date, as we are not counting the midnight Chinese restaurant in Soho where we drank wine from a teapot with friends. We would have counted it but none of us can remember any more than that, and my wife has asked me not to mention the fact that I invited eleven people into our hotel room the next morning to say hello. So without telling you any of that… our first official date was to a lovely restaurant in Essex where I spent two and a half hours on the phone to another woman. Guys you've either got it or you haven't—ouch—no seriously I thought that I would put the relationship to the test and all I can say is that she came through with top marks. I came through it with marks as well, but that's another story.

You have stood by me through a lot of decisions since we got together. You agreed to make me the happiest man in the world today and have a natural way that makes every day a joy to be with you.

I know that I told you earlier but I want everyone to know how beautiful you look today. Your dress is stunning and you really do look like a little princess. I can't wait to tell everyone that you are now my wife at every opportunity. I don't have to hope that our future together will be a happy one, I know it will be, because every day I wake to find that I love you twice as much as the day before. As my wife will tell you I'm often wrong, but in marrying her, I know I've made the right decision. Thank you darling.

I want to say a thankyou to our ushers for doing such a great job for us today. You have have done everything that we needed.

I am going to struggle to put this next part of my speech into words. There is someone else in this room that I love as dearly as my wife…and that is my son. Daddy is so proud of you and loves you so much. I cannot thank-you enough for agreeing to be one of my two best men today. You have given me so much joy and happiness and I want to reassure you that we will be there for you whenever you need us.

I remember the day that I took you to school and asked you whether you would mind if Daddy asked his girlfriend to marry him. You told me that it would be "really cool" and gave me a big hug. Well…it might have only been a few hours but I agree…it is "really cool."

It is an amazing feeling knowing how well you and my wife get on and I know how much you both love each other. I too love you with all my heart and we will try and give you the same support and guidance that we have had from our families. You are always going to be special in my eyes and that will never change.

And if your uncle has given you any stories to tell about your dad then you'd better forget them quick.

Oh dear…that brings me on to the other best man. Well…the best I could get at short notice. Thirty years of pain and misery he has caused me. He handed me a whole script of wonderful comments that I should tell you about him. Unfortunately, all this did was reinstate my belief of the fact that he is a compulsive liar and anything that he tells you should not be believed for one moment. I will confirm that he was in a different reform school to that of myself, so he knows nothing of the truth that went on in my childhood. He was only on day release during our teens and was back under lock and key before dusk, so he knows nothing of my underage drinking habits. Oops, sorry Mom!

The *[name of prison]* have been his home for the last fifteen years following the discovery that he is an absolute whiz at being able to forge photographic evidence. He would never have been found out had it not been for the fact that someone spotted his head on the new £20 notes instead of the Queen.

Well, hopefully that leaves you with nothing left to say…if not I'm sorry but can my family leave the room now.

Seriously, I could not think of anyone I would rather be best men for my wedding…no seriously I couldn't…I tried…but they were all booked. You have both affected my life in such positive ways and for that I am hugely indebted. We would like to show our appreciation for everything you have done today, and in the build up to the wedding, and have a small gift for you both. *[Present gifts]*

Now before I finish and ask you to join me in a toast, I believe that my lovely wife would like to gatecrash these speeches and say a few words.

[The bride's speech]

Thankyou darling.

I would like to bring my speech toward a close by saying a very special thankyou to our lovely bridesmaids.

I am sure you will all agree on how beautiful they look and I will always treasure the picture in my mind of you both entering the room and walking down the aisle. I would like you to know that your earrings and necklaces are a token of our appreciation for everything you have done today.

On that note, I would like to propose a toast to the bridesmaids, so would you all stand and raise your glasses and join us as we toast. To the bridesmaids.

Bride Speeches

⟨✦⟩

*V*ery often on the wedding day, some members of the wedding party may find themselves in the position where they feel either obliged or wanting to say something that was previously unplanned. This is a more common occurrence for the bride than anyone else. While you may not think that you will want to say anything, on the day you never know quite how you are going to feel. For this reason, it is well worth having a look at the example speeches on the following pages. Who knows, on your big day, something that you read in the next few pages might just stick in your mind and come in very useful when you least expect it.

Although it is by no means uncommon any more—the bride's speech is still a new development in terms of wedding procedure. If you do decide to make a speech, you can view the fact that this is not expected as a great advantage. Whereas the other main speakers have speaking roles with traditions attached to them—father is sentimental about daughter, best man gives groom a humorous character assasination—you and your speech are under no such expectations. You can more or less include what you like in your speech, it's entirely up to you.

If your father is not present, then you may want to speak first of all. You may prefer to speak after, or before, your husband, or even after the best man, as the very last speaker. The choice is yours, just as long as everyone knows when they are to deliver their speech.

Some couples may decide to speak together and others prefer to speak separately. The content of the bride's speech is entirely flexible, but here are some ideas to include:

* Thank the people who've supported you during the wedding.
* Thank everyone who's attending, especially friends you haven't seen for a long time and people who've traveled a long way.
* Thank guests for their gifts.
* Thank your mom.
* You could describe how you met your husband, your first impressions; how the relationship developed; your thoughts on love and marriage.
* You could thank the bridesmaids, rather than letting the groom do it.
* End with a toast to the guests.

Bride Speech – Example 1

The following speech was written, delivered by, and reproduced with the kind permission of Nancy Mirchandani.

The first of the example bride speeches is a short one and, as you will see, the bride has used the opportunity just to say thank you to everyone there. It is short, sweet, and to the point.

> We feel privileged to be sharing our day with all of our friends and families who have been important to us during our lives. Many of you traveled from afar: Canada, Seattle, Illinois, Colorado, and Arizona. Thanks to all of you for the efforts and sacrifices you have made to be with us today.
>
> I want to thank the most wonderful parents a child could ever have. Not only for the love, support, and guidance over the years, but also for everything you've done toward today. Your massive contribution has been priceless and without you both we would have never managed, and today would not have been possible or so special. Thank you mom and dad from the bottom of our hearts. And thank you *[groom's mom]* for having such a wonderful son.
>
> I would also like to say thank you to my beautiful bridesmaids. Thank you so much for everything you've done and for being the greatest friends ever. To my maid of honor, you have been a lifesaver. You truly are the definition of a best friend and sister. Thank you for dealing with all my indecisiveness and always being here for me. I want to thank my husband for making my life

complete. I am so lucky to be your wife and I look forward to spending the rest of my life with you. Lastly, we would like to thank each and every one of you for being here with us on this special day. Thank you. *[Toast]*

Bride Speech — Example 2

The following speech was written, delivered by, and reproduced with the kind permission of Beverly Buck. As you will see, more often than not, when a bride makes a speech at her own wedding, she normally takes the opportunity to thank everyone that has helped her, not just with the day but with her life in general. In a bride's speech humor is not necessary, however most brides cannot resist the opportunity of a couple of funny lines.

I wouldn't want anyone to think that I'm trying to have the last word here but I thought it only appropriate that the bride speaks and those of you who know me well enough will agree that it's usually hard to keep me quite. Well today is no exception, so here we go!

I feel privileged to be sharing our day with most of the friends and family who have been important to us during our lives. Many of you have traveled from afar: South Africa, Botswana, and even the UK, and some of you have had to take time off work to be here. Thanks to all of you for the efforts and sacrifices you have made to be with us today.

Of course there are those who are unable to be with us and there is one person in particular who I would dearly have loved to be here today to see me married and that is my dad. He's certainly been in our thoughts today, as he is everyday.

I'd like to thank the groom for his earlier compliments and would like to add how wonderful he looks today. We have been together for about fourteen years (as has been mentioned a number of times tonight) and during that time we've been through a lot. But he has many wonderful qualities: charm, brains, and beauty are sadly the only ones missing! No, seriously, I would like to thank him for being the person that he is. He is good company—funny, affectionate, and loving—a friend as well as a partner, and it means a lot to be his wife after so many years. I would now like to drink my own private toast to him and our future together. To the groom, you know everything about me and love me just the same.

Now I don't mean to bore you with repetition but I would like to say a few personal thankyous to some very special people who have contributed enormously to our day. Firstly, to the most wonderful mother a child could ever have—not only for all the love, support and guidance over the years but also for everything you've done toward today. Your massive contribution has been priceless and without you we would never have managed and today would not have been possible, never mind so special. Thank you mom.

A big thank you to my mother-in-law for the beautiful cake and for putting up with me changing my mind so often. I also understand you've trained your apprentice well, thanks to my mom for helping out. Thanks too to both my mother and father-in-law for their help and contribution toward today.

Special thanks to my gran for arranging the ceremony; to my grandad for proudly walking me up the aisle (keeping me at the right pace); to the organ player for keeping us all in tune in the church (well some of us); and to our friend for offering us the use of his luxurious car (which certainly beat the donkey and scotchcart we'd resigned ourselves to).

Thanks to all our attendants for agreeing to play their roles today—you've all done us proud.

My brother, who I've obviously known all my life and who I drove mad as a little sister (not to mention the time I drove him into the lemon tree on a motorbike—something he'll never let me forget!)

My niece and nephew, who I'm sure you'll all agree both look and have been brilliant. And last but not least, thank you to *all* our family and friends (there's too many to mention by name) for your help and support to our special day. Thank you for being here, we're having a wonderful time and hope you're all enjoying it too. Thank you.

Bride Speech – Example 3

The following speech was written, delivered by, and reproduced with the kind permission of Kelly Lewis.

You will see from the previous two examples that brides' speeches are normally quite short. It is not however a given rule that they have to be, as you will notice from the next example. A speech can be as long as you like. This speech flows very well from one line to the next and contains everything that is needed to make a perfect bride's speech.

This speech is more than just saying thank you, it also includes a description of when she first met the groom. Ending with a poem is a good way to conclude a speech, especially if you want to express something that you find difficult to put into words.

> You may well be wondering what the bride is doing making a speech. Well, those of you who know me well, know that I always have talked too much and usually find a way to get my say, so it probably isn't any surprise! I also wanted to say thank you to those deserving in my own words.
>
> When I met the groom, I was totally off men and relationships, so it is more than a little surprising to find myself standing here in this clobber just under two years later! I have my sister to thank for this remarkable conversion, as she was the matchmaker wannabe who got us together—with all the subtlety of *Blind Date* I might add. Her favorite trick was to invite the groom to

come for drinks with her and me and then suddenly "remember" she'd left the iron on or hadn't fed the cat or any other such nonsense.

Of course this was highly embarrassing and cringe-making but I am so very grateful to her for knowing us both better than we knew ourselves, knowing that we should be together and putting us in each other's lives.

She has been a great bridesmaid and she has helped a lot over the last few months; not least in the organization of a top hen party—the details of which follow the time honored code of, "What goes on tour, stays on tour!" She not only is the best sister a girl could ever have but she is also my very bestest friend and has been my idol since I arrived in this world. Thank you so much for everything, not least for loving me. This *[present]* is just a small gift as a token of our love and appreciation.

While I am on thanking there are a few more that I would like to do and I promise to be brief.

Firstly, thanks to all of you for coming and thank you for the wonderful gifts. We'll look forward to opening them when we get back from honeymoon. I know that most of you took time off work and traveled a long way to be here and I want to say how much it means to us to share our day with the family and friends that love us. Sadly not everyone could be with us and will be sorely missed here today.

Secondly, I want to thank the best best man—he has done a fantastic job, although, depending on the contents of his speech, I may retract this! Seriously, he has been an amazing support to the groom and has done us both proud in his role. Thanks for making our day that little bit more special and for not shaving the groom's hair off on the stag night.

Thanks also to my wicked step-mother! The reading was beautiful. Thank you for agreeing to do it. Thanks also for getting my father here on the right day, at the right time, and in the right clothes. Here's a little something for you to thank you for everything.

I'd like to say a few words about my mom and dad. They have been the best parents a girl could wish for and they are also my friends. My mom is the most amazing person and she taught me to be independent from a very young age. I'm sure the groom would *not* thank her for this as I am incredibly stubborn as a result, but it always made me aware that when I did get married, if I got married, it would be to the right man at the right time and that is certainly true. She is also an incredibly talented singer, which I'm sure those of you who heard her sing while we signed the register earlier will agree. It was beautiful and meaningful and I'll remember it forever. Thank you so much Mom. This *[present]* is a little gift from us.

My dad, on the other hand, taught me something that is invaluable: *sport is very important.* This is something that I know will stand me in good stead in my marriage! It is said that you marry a man like your dad and if that's true—then kind, generous, loving, caring, supportive, always there when you need him, and great to hug is what I'm getting. Thanks so much for everything dad, not least for giving me away—although you were probably glad to get rid of me!

I'd just like to say a few words about three of the most excellent girls and friends one could ever hope to meet. I've been very lucky to find friends like them. I just wanted to thank you all, not just for the practical things you have done, but for the support you have given me. These small gifts are a huge token of my love and appreciation.

So now I turn to my new husband! Last but certainly not least. I want to thank you for a wonderful day. Thank you for all your hard work in realizing our dreams; today has been so perfect.

I have never been able to find the right words to express just how I feel about this man who has become my husband today, so I'm going to recite this poem in the hope that it might go someway to let him know just what he means to me.

> I love you, not only for what you are, but for what I am when
>   I'm with you.
> I love you, not only for what you have made of yourself, but
>   for what you have made of me.
> I love you for the part of me that you bring out.
> I love you for putting your hand into my heaped up heart
> And passing over all the foolish weak things that are held
>   dimly there.
> And for drawing out into the light all the beautiful belongings
> That no-one else had looked quite far enough to find.
> I love you because you have helped me to make my life a

beautiful life worth living.

I love you because you have done more than anything could

have done to make me good

And more than any fate could have done to make me happy.

You have done this by being yourself and loving me.

You know, my gran always told me to marry a rich man—I couldn't have married a richer man. He is rich in inner strength, understanding, and kindness, in forgiveness and patience. He is my everything and I am very proud to be his wife. I'd like to propose a toast to us—the best is yet to come.

Bride Speech–Example 4

The following speech was written, delivered by, and reproduced with the kind permission of Kay Thomson. It is a short speech, very much to the point and perfectly written. Ironically, it is often the speeches that are well written as opposed to those that are not so well written that are the most difficult to read out. It is difficult to speak when you have a "lump" in your throat.

It is not traditional for the bride to speak but I thought it only right that I start married life by having the last word and I would like to take this opportunity to thank several people. Firstly, thank you for biting the bullet, proposing, and turning up today, on time and appropriately dressed. You are the love of my life, my best friend, and now my husband. I don't think anybody could be happier than I am today, and I can't wait for us to share the rest of our lives together. It means a lot to be your wife, after five years of being your girlfriend, and I'm sure he's happy now that he can start to let himself go.

To my in-laws, thank you for making me feel so welcome in your family. Thank you for raising him so well, although I understand that the warranty is out of date now and the refund deadline has long since passed. I might keep him for a while though as he has so many qualities: charm, brains, and beauty are sadly the only ones missing.

To dad and mom, thank you for your love, support and care over the last twenty-eight years and also for the generous financial contribution toward this wedding that helped us push the boat out a little further.

I feel privileged to be sharing our day with most of the friends and family who have been so important to us. Many of you have traveled from afar: Australia, Azerbaijan, Nigeria, Singapore, Germany, the UK, and some of you have had to take time off work to be here. Thanks to all of you for the efforts and sacrifices you have made to be with us today.

There are those who are unable to be with us and there is one person in particular who I would dearly have loved to be here today to see me married and that is my mom. She's certainly been in our thoughts today, as she is everyday. On that note I would like to propose a toast to absent friends.

Bride Speech—Example 5

The following speech was written, delivered by, and reproduced with the kind permission of Jane Dunn.

It is another short speech and mostly consists of thanking the relevant members of the wedding party and giving a personal message to the groom.

Anyone who knows me well enough will know that it is hard to keep me quiet and today is no exception—I thought it only appropriate that the bride speaks, although I promise to keep it short!

The main reason I wanted to make a speech was to personally say thank you to some very special people who have contributed to today.

[To the groom] Firstly, and most importantly, you've made me so happy since we met two years ago and today is the happiest day of my life. Thank you for making my life complete. Knowing your track record at either missing weddings or forgetting (or losing) your suit, I should also thank you for turning up at the wedding (eventually!) where we met, and, more importantly, thank you for getting to the church on time today and in your suit.

I would also like to say a big thank you to my bridesmaids. Firstly, my sister, for looking after me today and also on my hen weekend! Thanks very much for arranging our weekend in London, I'm sure everyone will agree we had an excellent time and I have a little something for you as a small token of my appreciation. And of course my other gorgeous bridesmaids who've been little angels today. I have a little something here for you both too. Thank you very much.

[Presents gifts]

I would like to thank my mom for all her help and support not just today but over the years and for giving me my "something old" which I'm wearing for luck today. I have a small gift from us for you.

I couldn't have been luckier to have such wonderful in-laws, thank you for making me feel so welcome in your family and for all your support with the wedding arrangements. A special thank you to my mother-in-law for sorting out the bridesmaids outfits and for making all of the invitations and order of service cards which were beautiful. And to my father-in-law, thank you for your lovely reading in church today. We also have a small gift for you both.

I would also like to thank all my friends who have who have contributed to today and helped with the arrangements. Thank you so much to all my wonderful friends for their friendship over the years. They have always been there for me when I really need them.

Lastly, thank you to everyone for coming today to celebrate with us, I hope you all enjoy yourself.

Father of the Groom Speeches

$\mathcal{I}$t is unusual for a father of the groom to make a speech, but the following example is an exception and illustrates that it is possible for any member of the wedding party to make a speech if they so desire. This type of speech would normally follow the groom's or bride's speech, but the order of speeches can be whatever is felt to be suitable, just as long as everyone knows who is speaking and when.

The involvement of the parents of the groom in the wedding can vary tremendously depending what jobs have been allocated to the bride's parents and what the bride and groom have decided they want to do themselves. Depending on your involvement, as the father of the groom you may feel that you would like to make a speech even if it is merely to offer congratulations, a toast, and some support for your son.

Father of the Groom

The following speech was written, delivered by, and reproduced with the kind permission of Bob Ross.

It is written with a lot of heartfelt meaning and is an excellent example of a reasonably short but flowing speech. There is a small amount of humor at the beginning and toward the end of the speech, but it is the sentiment that makes it special. The speech ends with some advice for the bride and groom, which is touching, and a toast in the form of a poem.

The happy couple, reverend celebrant, dear guests. The first wedding speech I ever gave was in 1958 when I married the groom's mother.

Oh, I was in love! I remember clearly what a great feeling courtship gave me. I used to lie awake all night thinking about something she said. After we married and had four kids I'd fall asleep before she finished saying it.

I'd like to focus on my son for a moment. He's married now, this may be his last chance to be the center of attention.

His arrival on this earth was a most significant event for us as his safe delivery was my wife's first after many disappointments. He was both long-awaited and much-wanted. Other birth disappointments followed but where there is a strong desire for offspring there is a way and eventually we were blessed with four lovely children. And they in turn have given me grandchildren who give me great pleasure.

When you are raising your kids you often wonder if you are getting it right. Forgive my little boast, but when I see how my children have turned out, it's all been worthwhile. Every one of them, their partners, and my grandchildren are worth knowing.

My son did not get the best start in life, losing his mother when he was sixteen years of age. Having me as a father did not always help. Few fathers are equipped to be mothers too, to bridge the gap successfully.

His mother and I felt he got every one of the personal qualities of both of us. Some of his good character came down through his genes. One rarely hears the word character mentioned these days, but what is important to this father is that he has it in abundance. He is loyal, hard working, conscientious, and faithful. He won't let you down. He has many good mates, some he has had for years and years, even dating back to his school days.

Two other indicators of his character worth mentioning are, first, that most of his personal development, both physically and intellectually, is a result of his own efforts. His extensive tertiary education was at his own expense and he is indeed an educated man.

The second indicator is the effort he has put into every gift he has ever given any member of his family, including six nieces and nephews while he had no children of his own. As a male it could easily have been a cop-out for him. But it wasn't, ever. I am very proud of him. I don't know the bride nearly as well, but I am a keen observer of the human condition and she strikes me as mature minded and capable, she carries herself well and, as a bonus, she comes from a loving family. Marriage is a balancing of attributes and from what I have seen the balance between this couple is sound.

Anyway, the fact that she chose my son as her husband and made him happy are good enough for me. It is good to see so many of their contemporaries here today. One tries to keep up as the world spins on its axis and I do concede the value of having their friends well represented to witness the start of their new life together.

In an attempt to be "with it," it is traditional for the groom's father to offer the couple some worldly advice. First, marriage will teach him any qualities he is lacking. He will have plenty of opportunity in the future to observe that, if he had just stayed single, he wouldn't have needed any of them.

Second, good communication is important: Never go to bed in the middle of an argument, stay up and fight it out, I say! And always remember to be diplomatic and magnanimous in the morning when you allow the other one to do it your way.

[To the bride] If you want something from the groom, you've only to ask for it. He is a man, hints won't work.

[To the groom] You may prefer to make all of the major decisions in your marriage while your wife makes all of the day-to-day ones. And fair enough too! If this is how it turns out, though, check it out, you may find that all decisions have been of a minor nature.

Events like today's don't just happen. They take a considerable amount of hard work and organization and I commend the bride and groom for the effort they have made to ensure a day worth remembering. It's their day, they've worked hard, and done good.

What I wish most for them is that they be each other's best mate. You can have all the love in the world swirling through the ether, flashing lights, sky rockets and balloons going up, but unless your partner is your best mate, the one who is always there for you, the one most interested in what you think and say, you will be missing out on the best of life's greatest institution.

Would you please join me in this toast to the newlyweds:

May you live as long as you like, and have all you need for as long as you live,

May the road you choose be smooth, and your burdens light.

May your pleasure in each other, grow with your years together.

The bride and groom.

Bridesmaid Speeches

ometimes one of the bridesmaids or a maid of honor (a term used less often these days) may want to make a speech. This speech can be delivered before the best man's speech. A chief bridesmaid is usually the bride's sister or her closest friend and undertakes some of the same duties as the best man for the groom. Unlike the best man, however, she does not have to make a speech, nor is she expected to be humorous. As there are no traditions surrounding the bridesmaid's speech, it can contain whatever you feel is appropriate, including thanks, quotes, advice, toasts, and even poems.

Bridesmaid Speech

The following speech was written, delivered by and reproduced with the kind permission of Debbie E. Tait.

It is a fairly short speech but contains all the key elements of a wedding speech: humor, sentiment, and love. It is fairly short, but offers a few humorous sayings, advice for the bride and groom, and, at the end, a poem. Quotes and poems are a good idea to include in a speech that you want to keep short, after you have given your congratulations or offered a toast.

> Before I start I would like to say that the bride looks absolutely stunning, and the groom, well he just looks stunned.
>
> For those of you who don't know me I am the bridesmaid and for those of you who do, I'll have my usual, thank you very much.
>
> When the bride first asked me to be her bridesmaid I felt delighted but as the big day approached I was informed that I would be doing a speech and a toast. Being the shy and retiring type I was trying to think of ways of getting out of it, but have any of you ever tried saying no to the bride?
>
> Then I thought, what could I talk about? Like any self respecting thirty something, I did research and came up with some sayings that I would like to share with you:
>
> * Some say that marriage begins when you sink into his arms and ends up with your arms in his sink.

* Others would say that when a man holds a woman's hand before marriage, it's love, after marriage it is self-defence.
* They say that before marriage a man will lay awake thinking about something you said, after marriage he'll fall asleep before you have finished saying it.

Now, I'm sure that there are some of you out there that can relate to that. Before I finish, I would like to offer my own advice for a happy and successful marriage. Now just because I'm not married or never have been it doesn't mean to say I am now not an expert on it.

[To the groom]

1. Whenever you're wrong, admit it, whenever you're right, shut up.
2. The best way to remember an anniversary is to forget it just once.
3. Set the ground rules first and then do everything she says.
4. Road maps are a good thing.
5. Never forget the two most important sayings, "You're right dear" and "O.K. buy it."
6. Never be afraid that she will leave you, she has spent years training you and she won't give that up lightly.
7. Woman do really need a pair of shoes for every outfit.

So on that note before I get into any trouble, I'll propose the toast: To the bride and groom.

> A wedding day will be remembered
> For all the joy it brings
> A day of love and happiness
> Of vows and wedding rings
> A day of new beginnings
> Learning what love truly means
> Your wedding day is just the start
> Of many hopes and dreams.

Best Man Speeches

Like the groom speeches, you may notice a fair amount of repetition among the best man speeches. The reason for this is that quite often someone will have attended a wedding, heard a good line, and then quoted it at the next relevant opportunity. That funny line is then passed on and much like a good joke before very long has reached many ears and been used in many speeches.

While this may sound like a good reason not to use lines that appear in more than one of these examples, as one comedian often said "It's the way I tell 'em!" If delivered correctly, no matter how many times you may have heard a funny story, if it is relevant to the situation and environment you will still find it amusing. The average person doesn't attend too many weddings and is therefore unlikely to have heard the jokes or stories before. Unless you know otherwise, you should work from the belief that you are talking to a "virgin" wedding reception audience.

More modern weddings have started to feature "best woman's" speeches, so we have included a good example at the end of this chapter.

Best Man Speech – Example 1

The following speech was written, delivered by, and reproduced with the kind permission of Findlay Black.

The speech is one of the best ones I have come across. It contains humor in abundance and is very skillfully written so that it gently flows from one sentence to the next. Not much of the speech contains moving or sentimental lines, but it does contain reminders of the high esteem in which the best man holds the groom. The speaker has decided to use visual props throughout the speech (photographs of the groom), which is an excellent way of adding humor and including the audience. As well as more general jokes, he has also incorporated some personal reminiscences to make the speech more individual.

" The hotel management have asked me to ask you not to stand on the tables or chairs during the standing ovation at the end of my speech.

Now, I asked around for an idea of how long my speech should last and the general response was about as long as it takes the groom to make love. So with that in mind, thank you, you have been a wonderful audience. *[Sit and then get back up]*

I think an introduction is worthwhile. For those of you who do not yet know me my name is Whatwouldyouliketodrink. I hope as many of you will come and say hello at the bar later, but I do insist you use my full name.

At this point I would like to thank the groom for his kind words. I would also like to add my own appreciation. I think you'll all agree the bridesmaids both look lovely today in their dresses and I know the bride wants me to thank them for the help they have provided, not only today but in the weeks and months leading up to the wedding. I would like to propose a toast. Ladies and gentlemen, the bridesmaids.

I'm sure a number of the guys here today have been a best man at a wedding before, but I wonder how many of you have ever received written guidelines from the bride to be. I would like to read you an e-mail that the bride sent me prior to the wedding: *[Produce email]*

Wouldyoulikeanotherdrink (Remember that is my name)

I was very pleased when you were asked to be best man at our wedding. I have known you for some time now and I cannot think of anybody more charismatic, intelligent, better looking or downright sexy than you to fulfil this crucial role on our big day.

As we get close to the wedding day, most tasks have been taken care of but there are two areas that do cause me a little concern—your speech and your conduct. I appreciate that as best man you are required to write a speech that pokes a certain amount of fun at my future husband, with stories and jokes about his past exploits, but I do want you to remember that this is our wedding day and I don't want something that you might say or do to spoil it.

With this in mind, please take note of the following and I'm sure we'll all have a wonderful day:

1. Do not get drunk.
2. Do not use bad language.
3. Do not tell dirty jokes.
4. Do not sing.
5. Do not let the groom sing.
6. Do not mention the groom's little problem .
7. Do not let the groom drink tequila.
8. Do not let the groom drink whiskey.
9. Do not let the groom drink.
10. Finally, make sure you keep your clothes on and make sure the groom keeps his clothes on.

> Love,
>
> The bride

Now while I cannot promise to keep to each of these demands, I have tried to take the responsibility of best man very seriously indeed. I would like to share with you some of my duties I have been involved with. One of my first tasks was to help get the groom fitted for a kilt. We had arranged to meet up at the kilt hire shop and I was running a little late so when I arrived he had already chosen a kilt. "What's the tartan?" *[pronounced Tart–in]* I asked to which he answered "Oh, I'm pretty sure the bride will be wearing a dress."

Another of my tasks was the potentially delicate duty of keeping the groom's ex-girlfriends out of the way today. Thankfully this has been made a lot easier for two reasons: 1. There aren't that many frankly and 2. Since the sheep epidemic last year, those exes that have not been culled are restricted by the quarantine laws in force.

Finally, it was my job to ensure the groom made it to the church fit and proper, on time and sober. As you can see this was achieved. To make sure this was the case, he stayed with me last night and I can assure you he was in bed early and he slept like a baby—that is, he wet the bed twice and woke every hour crying for his mommy.

During my research into weddings in general I looked into what are known as the "three key elements of the wedding ceremony" which can be summarized as follows:

1. The Aisle: it's the longest walk you'll ever take.

2. The Altar: the place where two become one.

3. The Hymn: the song we all sing to celebrate the marriage.

I can only assume the bride has read the same book, because as she stood before the minister I heard her whisper, "Aisle-altar-hymn, aisle-altar-hymn."

I think it is now time to give you all a run down on the chap who has tied the knot today. A kind of *This is Your Life*.

The groom was born on the April 1, 1968 and was about the size of a small baby. How times change! This was obviously April Fool's day and for what has followed, there can surely be no more appropriate entrance than that. It's a little known fact that the groom was nearly called Thursday. When he was born and presented to his father, he looked at him and said to his mother "I think we'd better call it a day!" I'm afraid to say I don't think he was the bonniest baby, because his mother's morning sickness didn't start until after he was born!

I didn't know him during his school years, but I'm reliably informed that he was not like the other five year olds when he started school—he was eleven. I managed to unearth an old report card which read "He is an ideal pupil who excelled in most subjects." However, on closer inspection it is clear the card has been doctored from its original state when it read: "He is an idle pupil who should be expelled from most subjects."

It may surprise you to know that the groom was very sporty at school—he now has the body of an athlete. I believe he keeps it in a tank of formaldehyde in his spare bedroom.

It was at this early age that he began his love affair with hair dye and he has experimented through the years. Here we see him trying out some ginger dye. *[Produce school photo]* Today it is clear he has chosen an unusual shade of gray.

Growing up, he became, as we all do, very interested in playing and watching soccer. He often played in the street and parks with his friends. Unfortunately he was then, as he is now, hopeless in every position. I suppose we should hope that the bride has better luck!

When the groom left school he took a joinery apprenticeship. He worked (I use that term loosely) for the district council then traveled the country shopfitting and he now works for his brother-in-law. I asked if his brother-in-law would like to comment on his employee. He was quick to tell me the groom is known as God at work. Knowing the groom as I do, this surprised me until he explained the reasons for the nickname:

1. You never see him.

2. He makes his own rules.

3. If he does any work, it's a miracle.

Like many young men still living at home, he caused his mom and dad some anxious times. In particular he would finish his dinner and sprint up Carlisle Road night after night. They feared the worst as he returned with a messy face and a glassy-eyed look. Had their youngest been taking drink or drugs? It soon became clear though that it was just his legendary craving for chocolate. He was paying his nightly visit to the local gas station (known as the Jet) that had an awesome array of chocolate and candies. Thereafter this stash of nightly goodies became known as the Jetpack *[produce and wear Jetpack—a collection of candies and chocolates]*. So here's one I prepared for the groom in case the hunger pangs strike later.

Today is one of the few occasions you will see the groom smartly turned out. The fashion disasters are too many to recall but to give you an idea this photograph shows him ready to go for a beer. *[Produces a photo of the groom dressed as a wizard.]* Baseball caps became quite fashionable but he never quite got the hang of it! *[Produces a photo of the groom in stupid hat.]*

There was a group of us who went through our twenties together having a laugh, a few drinks, and a dance. He was good at the drinking—his catchphrase being "Whose round is it?" or "Get to the bar" but rarely has anyone hit the dancefloor with such little regard for style or rhythm. He doesn't so much dance as jog. Indeed it has been estimated that during a twelve-inch remix he can cover upward of three and a half miles.

The script was similar for each of us. Even just having a girlfriend seemed to bring unnecessary grief. We'd meet a girl who seemed alright. We'd go out with them for about five months or so and then the nagging would start… "I want to know your name… I want to know your name."

Then came that fateful night. The bride is said to have remarked that she thought the groom was "handsome from afar," however earlier today she told me that she had actually said he was "far from handsome."

Things moved along nicely between them, everyone had their fingers crossed for the happy couple. Then in a restaurant one day the groom bent down to tie his shoelace, the bride jumped to conclusions and here we are today. The groom is not always the most romantic of characters. This is illustrated by the fact that his suggestion for the first dance tonight was "Stuck in the Middle with You." *[To the bride]* You are a lucky, lucky girl! I have to say *[to the groom]*, you have married a beautiful, intelligent, talented, and exceptional woman. *[To the bride]* I have to say, you have married *[the groom]*!

I would now like to read a few letters. I just hope no one has used joined up writing. *[Reads five letters that are genuine then one spoof]*

"To a loyal and valued customer, our very best wishes to you and yourbride. Will you be renewing your subscription?" (*Big & Bouncy* magazine.)

Obviously my toasts are going to focus on the most important people here today. The people we all feel a great love for and without whom today wouldn't be possible. At some stage in the evening I'm sure we will all be sharing with them our thoughts from this special day and giving them our love and best wishes so I would like to propose a toast to: the bar staff.

Now the real version. I would like to thank the groom for asking me to be his best man. It has been a pleasure helping them prepare for today. For all the banter that has passed between us it should be fairly obvious that we are the best of mates. I am going to finish now by asking you to join me in wishing them many years of happiness. Ladies and gentlemen, the bride and groom. That's the end of my speech. I am sure you will be as glad as me that there is no more.

Best Man Speech–Example 2

The following speech was written, delivered by, and reproduced with the kind permission of Dave Dundas. It is a superb speech, however it is best used by a best man who is either known for telling good jokes (and telling them well) or who at least has a lot of confidence as there are a lot of "one liners" contained within it.

> Good afternoon Ladies and Gentlemen. I am going to keep this speech fairly short because of my throat; the bride said that if I made fun of the groom too much she would cut it.
>
> Firstly, on behalf of the bridesmaids, I would like to thank the groom for those kind words and gifts. As I'm sure you will all agree, they all look absolutely beautiful and have carried out their role splendidly, so I think a round of applause for the bridesmaids is definitely in order.
>
> Just before I start the groom's character assassination, the bride was telling me earlier in the day that her pharmacy was broken into last week. The thief apparently stole ten boxes of condoms and ten boxes of viagra. The police are now looking for a hardened criminal.
>
> Next day a woman walks into the shop and asks her for some bottom deodorant, puzzled she replies, "I'm sorry we don't sell such a thing," "I beg your pardon" says the woman, "I buy it from here all the time." "Do you have the empty container from the last time," enquires the bride, "Yes I do," says

the woman and she walks out to her car, then comes back in with an empty deodorant stick." "This isn't a bottom deodorant madam, it's just a normal deodorant stick." The woman snatches it out of her hands and reads aloud, "To apply take off lid and push up bottom."

The groom was born in 1975, a year when the Khmer Rouge invaded Cambodia and Saigon surrendered to the North Vietnamese. So it's true what they say, these things always happen in threes.

He went to St. Serfs school were he was a rather quiet pupil, until of course, as anyone who knows him, he stepped onto the soccer pitch. He shunned the roll of forward for the more unorthodox "bare knuckle boxer" and "chief shin kicker" role, it was a novelty for him to be on the pitch a whole ninety minutes, never mind score goals. He then went on to play for Prestonfield Boys Club and then Napier University football team. Sadly this was to be the end of his sporting career, as this was when he discovered alcohol and women.

After school the groom worked in a Saturday job at Homebase. I spoke to an old work colleague who was only too happy to tell me of his time there. He also told me that he came to work one morning looking like he had never been to bed the night before, after about an hour his supervisor couldn't find him. After some investigation he found him sleeping in a bed display in the store room and, not be disturbed, he had even drawn the curtains.

After his time here he went to Telford, leaving with an HND in construction management. From there he went to Napier University where he graduated with a degree in building surveying. He then took a year out, traveling to Australia, where he worked on the new olympic stadium, learned to surf, and managed to kill one of Australia's rarest breeds of birds with the help of a rather large truck.

After returning to Edinburgh, he qualified as a chartered surveyor. This professional role gave him more opportunity to play golf. He was recently invited to play with the Edinburgh District Master Builders golf outing and was telling me he had overheard a discussion between four golfers. As three of the golfers went up to the tee they were boasting about their sons. The first golfer said, "My son is a builder and is doing so well he gave a friend a brand new house for free," "Well," said the second golfer, "my son owns a car dealership and he's doing so well he gave a friend two BMWs." The third man brags, "My son's a stockbroker and he recently gave a friend an entire share portfolio." Just as he finished the fourth man turned up on the tee, and the three golfers asked him about his son. "Oh," said the fourth man shrugging his shoulders, "my son's gay, but he must be doing something right as his last three boyfriends have given him a house, two BMWs, and a share portfolio."

The best man, as you all probably know, has several duties: helping to make sure things run smoothly on the day; keeping angry ex-girlfriends away; and watching out for the groom on the stag do, which I may add was in Amsterdam. I was doing plenty of watching, but not at the groom.

Now the groom has a reputation for being a bit tight and while we were in Amsterdam we saw a sign saying thirty guilders for super sex. "God," he said "there's no way I'm paying thirty guilders for a bowl of soup." We also went to watch blue movies, but he insisted on watching them backward so he could see the girl giving the money to the man.

While researching for this speech I found a quote that I thought was quite apt to the bride and my wife, who is due to give birth in ten days. "If you love something set it free, if it comes back it was and will always be yours. If it never returns, it was never yours to begin with. If it just sits in your flat, messes up your stuff, eats your food, uses the telephone, takes your money, and never behaves as if you set it free in the first place, you either married it or gave birth to it."

But remember, men are like a fine wine they start out like grapes and it is your job to stamp on them in the dark until they mature into something you'd like to have dinner with.

On the other hand, women are like a fine wine. They start out fresh, fruity, and intoxicating to the mind and then turn full-bodied with age until they go sour and vinegary and give you a headache.

I'm sure you'll all agree with me that the bride and groom make an absolutely beautiful and happy couple, so if you could charge your glasses and join me in a toast. To the bride and groom.

Best Man Speech – Example 3

The following speech was written, delivered by, and reproduced with the kind permission of Simon Chattel, who is the groom's brother. Prior to delivery, the speaker had a "couple" of beers. His advice after this experience is not to drink beforehand, as it made him feel even more nervous.

The speech makes use of a couple of visual props and begins with a familiar joke (about kissing the Queen) but continues the joke further when he reads out the cards. Even if you are using a popular joke, there is no reason why you can't adapt it for your own purposes.

Firstly, on behalf of the bridesmaids, I'd like to thank the groom for his kind words, and I have to say they have done an excellent job today and look absolutely wonderful.

I am very proud that I was chosen to be the best man today. It's often said at weddings that being asked to be the best man is like being asked to kiss the Queen. It's a great honor but nobody wants to do it.

I have a large library of stories to tell you that will leave the groom embarrassed and humiliated, but out of respect for him on his big day I have decided not to tell them. So I'm not going to tell you about the time he vomited over a taxi driver's head or ended up in hospital on his stag do.

The groom was born on November 13, 1972. Coincidentally, this was also the year that the first Mr. Men books were published, and if you know him or know anyone that has lived with him, you'll easily be able to guess which Mr. Man he takes after. No, its not Mr. Topsy-Turvey or Mr. Bump, it's Mr. Messy. Even though he stopped reading the Mr. Men books last year, I doubt he will ever loose his natural ability to make a mess. *[To the bride]* If you need any tips on getting him to tidy up, don't ask my mom or dad as they were unsuccessful for twenty years.

After leaving school, the groom had a brief career as an accountant but soon saw the light and decided that cleaning a swimming pool would be more interesting. After a few other career moves he decided that he was missing something, so decided to go to university to study sport science.

Before he'd gone away to university, the groom was extremely fit, as skinny as a rake, and very serious about his cycling. It was on the following Christmas holiday when I saw he was starting to put on a bit of weight that I realized—he'd fallen in love with beer. I hear he had an excellent time at uni, living in a house of like-minded people who also had this great love.

The stag do was a couple of weeks ago in Brighton and on the Saturday evening we went to a club called The Event. For those of you who don't know this club, it's described as giving you the most electrifying night of your life, and to see the groom dance there you'd think he was being electro-cuted. Unfortunately for the groom, several people had cameras and I have had some of the raunchier pictures blown up so you can all see what he got up to. A couple of people told me not to show them as it could spoil the bride's wedding day, but I know that she will understand. *[Shows pictures]*

143

Moving on to the happy couple. They met while working at a super-market but didn't officially start seeing each other for quite a while. Just over two years ago the groom ran the London Marathon. It was at the finish that emotion got the better of them. They ran into each other's arms and burst into tears. They had come to the marathon as close friends and I think probably left as an item and have stayed together ever since.

I would like to say how wonderful she looks and what a lucky man the groom is. They married today for better and for worse. The groom couldn't have done better and the bride couldn't have done… *[Look down at notes and stumble]* better either.

It's plain for all to see what the groom sees in the bride—sitting there all in cream—she's going to blend in nicely in their kitchen.

I'm now going to read out a few messages:

"I will leave the key to the palace under the backdoor mat."

Signed "The Queen"… Oh Sorry… that one is addressed to me. *[Pocket the card]* There were also one or two messages from some of the groom's ex-girlfriends *[pull out full black bin liner]* but I'll only read a couple.

"From all of us at Madame Thrashards Spanking Emporium, we hope you have a great day."

Here's another one: "I can't help thinking about what could have been. Loving you always. Tarquin."

Moving swiftly on. Could you all please stand now and join me in a toast. To the bride and groom's parents for this special day. Thank you. While you are all still standing, I'd like to say that it really has been an honor and a pleasure being best man, but today I am the best man in name only. It's the bride and groom's day and I'd like to wish them all the very best for this new chapter in their lives. Please join me in a toast. To the bride and groom.

Best Man Speech – Example 4

The following speech was written, delivered by, and reproduced with the kind permission of Jason Roos. It is a fairly short speech and contains a lot of meaningful and sentimental statements. While not every best man will look to write and deliver a speech with such feeling, if this is the type of speech you are looking for, this is an excellent example.

Good afternoon ladies and gentleman. I would like to echo the groom's sentiments and mention that all the bridesmaids look truly beautiful, indeed.

Also, I'd like to say that the bride looks absolutely stunning today, as for the groom he just looks stunned. I am on a strict time limit from the bride, so the more you laugh at my jokes, the quicker my speech will be.

It is beautiful to see so many loving family members and friends here to share in this occasion, especially those who have traveled some distances to be here with us today. For those of you who don't know me, I have been a friend of the groom's for seven years. He has many special friends, and having the privilege of being chosen as his best man, from such esteemed company, is an honor the likes of which I have never had bestowed upon me.

I like to think that my selection as one of the best men is not really because your other friend canceled on you, but because I am one of the few people in the room and indeed alive that has actually seen you hit a homerun.

To be called a best man on a day like this is somewhat of a paradox. For today belongs to only one man, and that's you. No matter the size and liberality of the thoughts and tokens provided to you today, you have already attained the greatest gift a man can wish for; the love of a woman as beautiful and caring as the bride.

I have had the distinct pleasure of knowing, for a considerable portion of my life, both of them individually, before knowing them as a couple. The beautiful girl that every boy in our class was madly in love with and the boy from the baseball team, who I didn't like much at the time. Spending time with the two of them is like slipping into a surreal realm where true love exists twenty-four hours a day, seven days a week. To see two people care for and adore each other as much as they do is something truly special. When all the wishes of good luck and happiness are forgotten after today, I have no doubt that the love you two have for each other will last you many lifetimes over.

Now would probably be a good time to bring up some dirt on the groom and tell you all how the bride has changed him into a better man and so on. Unfortunately this is not the vessel for those stories, however you can bid for them in drinks later on at the bar.

I was speaking to the bride's dad just this morning and he was saying how he can't believe how fast she has grown up. Just the other day he remembers her as a beautiful little angel, running around with a dummy and if we take a look today, not all that much has changed. I then asked the groom's mom if there were any cute photos I could talk about. She said there was one of the groom, crawling naked on a rug, playing with his toys, dribbling his chocolate biscuit everywhere, but we didn't think it was appropriate, as it was taken just after his 21st.

[To the groom] You leave here today having gained a wife that is warm, loving, and caring, a wife whose outer beauty is surpassed only by her amazing inner radiance.

[To the bride] You on the other hand, leave today with, well a gorgeous dress and a lovely, lovely bouquet. Charles Dickens said a measure of a woman's love for her man was the lengths to which she was prepared to go to make him happy. If this holds true, then you have reached that goal, for the groom is the happiest I have ever seen him. And if the groom is half as good a husband as he is a best friend, then you will have left here with a man that epitomizes honor and respect both and for himself and for those he loves.

As is customary, I should leave the groom with wise words, to help in your marriage. Since I am a bachelor, I have little experience to speak from, but I hope these help anyway:

1. Never go to bed angry; always stay up and argue.
2. Always remember those three little words that are so important in a marriage: "You're right dear."
3. Lastly, under no circumstances will you swear at your wife, if there are ladies present.

Searching around to find a pertinent closing thought, all were overshadowed by the validity of the following: "You don't marry someone because you can live with them, you marry them because you simply cannot live without them." Ladies and gentlemen, if you could all be upstanding and join me in a toast: To the two people who are so dear in all our hearts, the bride and groom.

Best Man Speech – Example 5

The following speech was written, delivered by, and reproduced with the kind permission of Phil Chaplow.

The speech presents the groom's life story in a brief and humorous way. You will see that this is quite a common thread in many speeches and using old school reports is a popular method of doing so.

Good afternoon ladies and gentlemen. It's surprising just how far some people are prepared to travel for a free lunch. It's a good job the groom didn't choose the menu, otherwise we would have had cheese sandwiches washed down with beer.

Firstly, I have a few messages to read out. *[read telegrams etc.]* As Henry VIII said to each of his wives, I won't keep you long.

I'd like to begin by thanking the groom for asking me to be best man. I would also like to thank the bride for allowing him to ask me. The groom has a splendid set of friends, and to be nominated from such esteemed company, is without doubt a great honor. Thanks also to the ushers, friends, and family who have all helped to make this day so special.

[To the bride] You make a fine bride and look beautiful and radiant. I couldn't help but notice the groom swell with pride when he saw you walking down the aisle in that dress. *[To the groom]* You are indeed a lucky man, you have married someone who is attractive, warm, loving and caring. A wife who

will be all you could ever wish for and more. *[To the bride]* You have married someone who is: handsome, witty, intelligent, charming, good looking… *[To the groom]* Sorry, I'm having trouble reading your writing.

When the groom asked me to be his best man I consulted the Internet for help. I discovered that the job is essentially comprised of four main tasks:

1. Organize the stag party (perhaps you could tell us again how you burst the inflatable sheep).
2. Help the groom dress (at last I found out where the G-string from Dublin went).
3. See that any ex-girlfriends are kept at bay (quite a task as most of them have been released under care in the community).
4. Make a speech. I thought it was going to be tough following a speech by the groom and I was right, I couldn't understand a single word he said.

I did find a lot of other interesting things on the Internet but I won't go into that now.

I met the groom over ten years ago, and I often wonder what it would be like if I didn't have him as a friend. Sometimes the smile lasts for days. He has more skeletons in his closet than Fred West ever managed.

I have plenty of stories that I could tell you about the groom, fortunately for him alcohol has blurred many of them, and the others are really unsuitable for this occasion. I'm sure that as today wears on then some of them may come out. The groom will perhaps tell you some himself, then I could fill you in with what really happened.

However, I feel obliged to give those of you who don't know him too well a brief rundown of his life so far, to give you an idea of what sort of person he is. He was born in 1973, the same year that Value Added Tax (VAT) was introduced in the UK, setting the tone for his popularity. Although his parents loved him, it's not hard to believe he was an extremely ugly baby. In fact I'm told his mom didn't start morning sickness until after he was born. He didn't enjoy school as much as the other kids. At playschool he was different, all the other kids were four years old and he was eight. But in his defense he was a special child, so much so that he was put in all the special classes. By the time he was nine he had started reading his first book and by the time he was fourteen he'd finally finished it. I have managed to obtain a copy of his school report. Obviously I wasn't at school with him, but you can imagine my surprise when I read his former teachers comments:

Geography: *[The groom]* is the only one in the class who thinks Ellesmere Port is a fine table wine.

Biology: While *[the groom]* is often enthusiastic he took it a little too far by revising for his blood test.

Religious Education: *[The groom's]* understanding of Christianity is very limited, so much so that he still believes the Book of Genesis was written by Phil Collins.

It was at School that he first met *[the bride]* and although there was mutual attraction it was to be a few years down the line before they were to fall in love. In the meantime he would find other ways of pleasuring himself.

Until then cars and alcohol were his passion and this is where we formed our close friendship. One time while servicing on a rally in the Middle East, the groom was propositioned for marriage by a rich Sheikh who took a fancy to the fresh-faced youth. I left them to it. I'm not sure what happened that night but the sheikh had a new boyfriend the next day. Perhaps the bride will be able to enlighten us there?

I will save stories such as when the groom went jogging round Kendal Parks naked, the crazed woman in Malta who gave him a little more that he bargained for (the pot of yogurt didn't expect that either), or the many other tales for another time.

After a few failed relationships (sixty-nine does indeed seem to be his lucky number), he was once again left looking for his soul mate. His long-term relationship with beer would always remain, but he needed someone else in his life.

When he met the bride in the local nightclub one night, the attraction he felt at school was re-kindled. He told me the following day how lucky he felt that his childhood dream was about to happen, a date with the bride. It was at this point I realized that this might be the girl he had been searching for, and today this has been proven. He was smitten like never before and made the choice to settle down with her. Together they chose a house with a lovely mature garden. His time spent admiring the garden enabled him to set up a part-time scrap metal business from the empty beer cans that quickly piled up.

I was talking to the bride before the wedding and asked her how she felt about sex before marriage. She replied it should be no problem, as long as it didn't hold the ceremony up too long. With an attitude like that then I'm sure that they will have a long and happy life together.

The groom has always been extremely generous and very loyal. He is also good company and great fun. I know that as a friend no one could wish for better, and he will offer even more to the bride.

Today is a day when each one of us wishes the happy couple well. Being human they will have their disagreements. Life being what it is there will be sad moments as well as glad. Yet I know that today we are all wishing them happiness and health in those years to come, and I am sure that the love between them will be strong enough to last forever. Here's to love, laughter, and happily ever after. As they start their new life let's toast the new husband and wife. To the bride and groom.

Best Man Speech – Example 6

The following speech was written, delivered by, and reproduced with the kind permission of Shane Green. The majority of the actual material contained within the speech is not original, however one of the reasons for including this speech is that the speaker has tied a lot of "borrowed" jokes together very well. You will be able to notice that he has slightly adjusted a few gags so that they suit the speech and the groom.

I would also like to thank you all for being here today to share in this very special occasion. As we have been eating our meal this afternoon, I have had time to look around the room at you all and have been struck by just how far people will travel for a free meal.

Before I begin my traditional destruction of the groom's character, I would just like to say again how lovely the bride looks today. This is actually the first time I have made a speech (as you can probably tell), and it is true when they say that it's nerve racking. In fact I would go so far as to say that I feel about as comfortable as Osama Bin Laden in the Whitehouse.

I only feel slightly better knowing that I am not the only one in the room who is apprehensive, but then again she has just married *[the groom]*. On the score of being nervous, I am sure that you have all heard the groom say over and over that he has not been at all nervous in the run up to today. Well, that all changed at about 9 o'clock this morning. I've known him for the best part of twenty-three years now and of course there are plenty of things I could tell you about what we were like as kids. Unfortunately, I did consult my solicitor and he tells me that we could still face prosecution, so maybe not.

The groom was born in the early part of 1973 and while I'm not saying that was an omen, events later that year included the oil crisis, the release of *The Exorcist*, and of course the introduction of Value Added Tax (VAT) in the UK.

His mom was only saying last night that he was a pretty baby who was often mistaken for a girl and that as a child he loved nothing more than sitting for hours staring blankly at the TV. No change there then mate!

At five years of age, the groom started at the same school as me. I remember that he loved soccer and tried for the school team on every occasion. Unfortunately, he was found to be useless in every position *(Turn to bride)*. Best of luck then!

As I got to know him, I realized that here was a man who thrived on daredevil sports and laughed in the face of danger. I tell you, in those days the groom with a hula hoop was a sight to behold.

As a kid he had a huge appetite for life, and this helped him become wise. Unfortunately, I just had a huge appetite and it only helped me to become wide. As we got older, we became inseparable, joined together with a bond too strong to break. And after that experience we never did sniff glue again. At eleven years old, he started at the big school. It was here that he got interested in girls clothes. *[Look puzzled]* Sorry, girls AND clothes.

I'm pleased to say that his school reports stated that "he is an ideal pupil who is a light unto others." *[Look puzzled again]* Sorry, That actually reads "he was an idle pupil who set light to others."

Fortunately, we made it through school with only a few minor blemishes along the way. Not least of which was when our English teacher tried to ban us from taking our exams because she said we were cheating. Personally I don't see what's cheating about using someone else's work when it's better than your own but still.

When he left school, the groom joined the R.A.F. and I'm sorry to say that for the following few years we all but lost touch, apart from a two week holiday in Majorca. Now, I'm afraid I can't go into too much detail about that as my mom is here, but for those of you who are interested there is a video and DVD available at the bar later.

On to more recent times… When he told me he was getting married I have to admit I was shocked. You see, I had already got to know the bride and had always thought she was quite intelligent. But here they are, married for better or for worse. Couldn't be more appropriate really, as he couldn't have done any better and she couldn't have done much worse.

Now, as I mentioned earlier this is the first time I have been a best man and not really knowing my responsibilities I bought a book for some advice. It told me that I had several major duties:

1. Make sure he gets a good night's sleep before the big day. I'm pleased to say that he slept like a baby—he woke up every two hours crying for his mom!

2. Look after the rings and get him to the wedding on time. Yep, managed that one.

3. Make sure his flies are done up. Sorry mate but you're on your own with that one!

4. Keep any angry ex-girlfriends at bay. The sheep epidemic saw to that.

5. Organize a stag do. Unfortunately, as the bride and groom seem to do things with virtually no warning, I didn't have time to arrange the traditional weekend in Amsterdam. I did, however, manage to book a few of us into a little restaurant I know where we had a pleasant hour or two and a small sherry to wish him luck! *[Turn to the groom and take money from him]*

For those of you who don't know, the bride and groom met in this very hotel. To spare him, I won't go into too much detail about the night apart from to say that it involved a lot of beer and a pair of black boxer shorts with holes in them. I am also reliably informed that their beautiful daughter was conceived here. Although I am assured it wasn't on the same night.

When they announced they were getting married I couldn't have been more pleased. He topped it off for me of course when he asked me to be his best man. *[To the groom]* I would like to say that you are my oldest and dearest friend. We have been through some bad times and we have been through a lot of good times. Your friendship has been a source of strength to me throughout the years and I want to say that it has been an honor and a privilege to stand beside you today, thank you.

I would also like to take this moment of seriousness to mention some-one very dear to the groom and, indeed, to many of us around the room, and that's his dad. Those of us who knew him knew just how much his family meant to him and how proud he would have been today. *[To the groom]* I'm sure that your dad would have loved today, and I know just how happy he would have been that you have found someone to share your life with.

Now, I am sure that you are all pleased to know that I am almost fin-ished. All that remains is for me to read out some of the beautiful cards that have been sent to the happy couple. *[Read cards]*

One final thing before I ask you all to join me in the final toast of the evening, my girlfriend has asked me to pass on some advice to you both. *[To the bride]* she says: "Remember that men are like tiled floors, lay them right the first time and you can walk all over them for years!" *[To the groom]* "Always have the last word in any argument: 'yes dear.' "

And for the final time this evening, would you all be upstanding and charge your glasses. To my best friend and his lovely new wife. May your love be modern enough to survive the times, but old-fashioned enough to last for ever.

Best Man Speech – Example 7

The following speech was written, delivered by, and reproduced with the kind permission of Richard Hall. While there are many good lines in this speech, I'm sure the one thing that it was best remembered for is the main story about the groom when he was just a boy. If you are feeling particularly nervous and do not feel comfortable telling one line jokes, a story such as this together with a few short lines about the happy couple can produce an excellent speech.

> Good afternoon ladies and gentlemen. Firstly, on behalf of the bridesmaids, I would like to thank the groom for his kind words, and may I also say that they have done a fantastic job today and all of them look absolutely beautiful.
>
> I'd also like to say that the bride looks absolutely stunning today as I'm sure you will all agree. Unfortunately, for the wedding photographs, the groom just looks stunned.
>
> When I was asked to be best man I consulted the Internet for help. I must confess I was perplexed by some of the things I was expected to do:
>
> Help the groom dress. Thanks, but no thanks. If he hasn't learned by now then he never will.
>
> That his shoes are tied.
>
> That his face and hair are "in order" (God didn't put them in order first

time round, I'm not convinced that I stood a chance).

That he has nothing between his teeth (or is that his ears?)

That his trouser flies are done up.

I came to the conclusion that best man is just a fancy title for nanny. I also found out some other interesting things on the Internet, but now is definitely not the time to tell you what they were.

However, I have taken the job of being best man seriously and have made sure:

That he got to the service on time.

That he was well dressed and looking smart, which I'm sure you will agree he is.

And that he got a good night's sleep last night, and I'm pleased to report he slept like a baby. He woke up every half hour like clockwork, crying for his mom.

So what can I say about the groom? Well, he's witty, intelligent, charming, successful, han... han... Sorry, I'm having trouble reading your writing.

I've been racking my brain for the last couple of weeks trying to think of suitable stories to be said about the groom today. I briefly flirted with the idea of recounting the stag night, but I quickly realized that if I did I would be beaten up by several people—so that idea disappeared very quickly.

His teenage years can be defined as several years of drinking and sleeping in the bathroom, cuddled up to the toilet bowl. It's good to know that some things never change.

At school, he tried many sports to no avail. When he tried rugby he was told his tackle was not big enough. He tried cross country running but could not stand the pace, and when it came to soccer he was useless in every position. Whether the bride can confirm those three things for us I don't know, but I hope she has more luck.

Now, of course, I'm not the only person in this room that he knows well. In fact, this place is stuffed with people that have an opinion of him. So, I thought it would be an idea to find out what some of you think of the groom, and share your thoughts at his wedding. Over the last few weeks I've been approaching his friends and colleagues. This is what just a few of you said. His boss (and I can quote him now as he's not here), said: "Working with him is like working with a God: He's rarely seen, he's holier than thou, and if he does any work it's a bloody miracle."

Another absent colleague, rang me the other day and said: "He's really looking forward to the wedding, and especially the honeymoon, he's been going on about it all week. One thing I can't understand though, is why he's taken to wearing fake tan to the office."

Unfortunately, he has also been described by someone as "arrogant, insensitive, and selfish." And let's face it, if anyone should know it's his mom. I had a long conversation with her to delve into his childhood, and unearth some embarrassing tales. If you are all sitting comfortably, then I shall begin.

At the age of seven or eight, possibly during the long summer holidays, he pestered the life out of his parents to stay in the back garden in their tent overnight. After going on and on all day, he eventually got his way and armed with toys, juice and cookies went to bed in the tent under one condition that he was not to come back in and out of the house all night and keep everyone else awake. Now, being seven years old, after drinking lots of juice and being all excited about sleeping in the tent in the back garden, nature called during the middle of the night. Remembering the rules, he didn't go back in the house to go to the toilet. Nor did he, as most of us would have done, get out of the tent and go in the garden. At this point I'd like to paint a picture for you all, and let's see his reaction.

I have here a bucket of Lego *[produce bucket]*. I also have a glass of water, and you've already guessed what's coming next. *[Pour water into bucket]* That done, I imagine he fell soundly asleep. Next morning, his childhood wisdom did not lead him to dispose of the contents of his Lego bucket in the garden. Nor even, down the toilet after packing up the tent and toys. Instead, the Lego bucket and it's unusual contents went up to Lee's bedroom. And stayed there for two weeks. One bucket, one wee, some floating Lego, and an incredible smell, as discovered by his mom a fortnight later.

I spoke to many people asking for their advice to give to you today. Rather than stand here for hours, I'll just give you the top three:

1. Set the ground rules and establish who's boss… and then do everything the bride says.

2. Never be afraid that she will leave you. She's spent years training you already, she's not going to throw that away lightly.

3. Never forget to say those three little words at least once a day for the rest of your life: "You're right dear."

As they say, a man who gives in when he is wrong is a wise man. A man who gives in when he is right is married.

We have had some great times together and I know that we will continue to do so in the future. You have been a great friend to me over the past few years, and you are one of the most genuine, most sincere, and unselfish people I have ever known, and it is truly a great honor to be your best man.

I'd like to say a few words about the bride now. I'm afraid I don't really recall the first time I met her, as it was one of the very rare occasions when I was slightly drunk. However, over the last year or two I've got to know her quite well. She is one of the most caring and kind people I have ever met and that is a quality that is so very rare. You are both very lucky people to have found each other.

Now, if you could join me in a toast to some very important people, without whom today just wouldn't be the same. I'm sure all of us at some point will shuffle past them and exchange a few kind words. Ladies and gentlemen, I'd like you to raise your glasses and say a toast. To the bar staff.

And of course we should not forget the bride and groom. I would like to say to you both: "May your love be modern enough to survive the times, and old-fashioned enough to last forever."

Today is a day when each one of us wishes the happy couple well. Being human they will have their disagreements. Life being what it is there will be sad moments as well as glad. Yet I know that today we are all wishing them happiness and health in those years to come, and I am sure that the love between them will be strong enough to last forever.

Ladies and gentlemen, the bride and groom.

Best Man Speech–Example 8

The following speech was written, delivered by, and reproduced with the kind permission of Scott Agass and Simon Middleton. Often, with so many good friends, the groom may find it difficult to select a best man. For this reason, it is becoming more and more common for there to be two best men. As you will see, a speech by two best men can work extremely well. Here, one speaker delivers a joke and the other delivers the punchline. It is also an excellent method of presenting visual jokes. It ends in a song; an excellent conclusion.

Best man 1: Good evening everyone, I must warn you we are both pretty nervous about doing this speech. We have spent many a night awake trying to plan it to no avail. We were both so nervous about doing this speech we asked the groom for some advice on how to prepare for talking to a large audience.

Best man 2: So he did. He told us to imagine that you are all naked, so if you
don't mind, we are going to give it a go. *[Stares, winks at people]*
Thanks for asking us to be best men, a lot of people have said to
us being a best man is a bit like sleeping with the Queen.

Best man 1: It's a great honor but nobody wants to do it!

Best man 2: Ladies and gentleman, may I thank you for attending this wonderful occasion. You can all agree that today has been a great success, so far, they look absolutely stunning. So if you could raise
your glasses. To the bride and groom.

Best man 1: Also, thanks must go to the beautiful bridesmaids, who did a fabu-
lous job today getting the bride ready and making sure she didn't
back out. So if you could please raise your glasses again. To the
bridesmaids.

In preparing for today the groom has given us a list of things we
have to do, so if you don't mind, for our sake and for yours, we
would just quickly like to run through it, sorry.

[Get pens and list out of pockets]

Make sure that the groom is dressed appropriately.

Best man 2: No better than usual, check. *[Pretends to check list]*

Best man 1: Ensure that the groom has been to the bathroom.

Best man 2: I made sure he went in there, but the rest was up to him!

Best man 1: See that angry ex-girlfriends are kept at bay.

Best man 2: Errrmmm, I can't find any, most of them seem rather relieved.

Best man 1: Bring a bag with the following items for emergencies.

Best man 2: Aspirin, antacid, deodorant, toothpaste, Viagra. Oh, sorry the groom wasn't going to mention that.

Best man 1: Get him to the wedding on time.

Best man 2: Oh, we're here, were doing O.K.

Best man 1: We'd like to take this opportunity to read a few cards that have been sent here today for the bride and groom. There seems to be just the two, both addressed to the groom. One reads, "We could have been so good together," Britney Spears. This one reads the same, "We could have been so good together," love, Elton John.

Best man 2: I have known the groom since the age of twelve when we first met at school and, like everyone at that age, he went through some fashion disasters. Remember the perm? But he never had a funny nickname at school that I can tell you about, or so I thought! He did have a nickname before the operation on his ears. Do you remember what it was? That's right "Wingnut" and here's why. *[Put on a mask]*

Best man 1: I first met the groom on a night out at the local night club known then as "5th Avenue" in the early 1990s. He was still a bit out of touch with fashion even back then. I remember after chatting to him for a while him asking me some advice on meeting women, the only chat-up lines he had were: "Here's some money, phone your mum and tell her you won't be coming home tonight."

Best man 2: And the other one he always used to use: "Please go out with me, I've never been out with a girl before." *[high pitched voice]*

Best man 1: Fortunately we changed him for the better into the ladies man he is today! *[Toast glasses]*

Best man 2: They were good times back then as you must remember, but paying for a night out wasn't easy so we all had to have some bad part-time jobs to pay for them, but not as bad as the groom's.

Best man 1: Chris did progress in his jobs though, he started off as a paper boy and moved on to picking up litter on the side of the road.

Best man 2: But that was a garbage job. He then had a job installing dodgy TV channels. For a while he worked at a supermarket on the cheese counter and then as a butcher.

Best man 1: But he got the chop from that! So he has tried many things but his real vocation in life was to do what he's doing today, and what a success he has been. He is now working for IBM as a business consultant after gaining a degree in home economics.

Best man 2: No, it was just economics. But there were a few times when we got a bit worried about his sexuality through his career, like the time he moved to live with two other guys.

Best man 1: What, when he moved to Camptown?

Best man 2: Well, he's always been into bodybuilding and he did always insist, on our nights, that we all slept in the camper van with him.

Best man 1: Did you find that you always woke up with your pants on the wrong way round, funny that. Chris, what can we say? Today you are the groom getting married to a wonderful bride and we have been bestowed with the honor of being your best men. Today you truly are the best man and I hope your love will be modern enough to survive the times and old-fashioned enough to last forever.

Best man 2: Ladies and Gentlemen. It gives me great pleasure, not to mention blessed relief, to ask you all to charge your glasses, once again be upstanding and raise a toast. Let's drink to love, which is nothing unless it's shared by two. Congratulations to the bride and groom.

Best man 1: To end we would just like to read a few verses from this poem that is very close to our hearts. It is called "The Power of Love" which was written by William Shakespeare.

Best man 2: Wasn't it also covered by Huey Lewis and the News in 1985 for the film *Back to the Future*?

Best man 1: Yeah O.K. quiet. *[Sing]*

The power of love is a curious thing

Make a one man weep, make another man sing.

Change a hawk to a little white dove

More than a feeling, that's the power of love.

Best man 2: It's O.K. mate

[Pats him on the shoulder] Let me:

You don't need money, don't take fame

Don't need no credit card to ride this train.

It's strong and it's sudden

and it's cruel sometimes

but it might just save your life.

That's the power of love, that's the power of love!

Thank you.

Best Man Speech–Example 9

The following speech was written, delivered by, and reproduced with the kind permission of Tony Bradley.

When making a speech it is often relevant to include a mention to a piece of current news or even an event that is in progress. This speech was given on the day that England were playing a game in the World Cup and the speaker makes reference to this early in the speech.

" On behalf of all the bridesmaids I would just like to thank the groom for his kind words. Can I say what a great job they've all done today and add how wonderful they are looking. The same must also be said about the bride. I think she looks absolutely stunning. And the groom, well he just looks absolutely stunned.

I'd like to begin by thanking him for asking me to be best man. I'd also like to thank the bride for allowing the groom to ask me. I've found out over the past few months that being asked to be a best man is like being asked to make love with the Queen. Its a real honor, but deep down, nobody actually wants to do it.

This is a beautiful wedding almost like a wedding on T.V. When the groom first informed me that he was getting married, my first reaction was to ask when the baby was due. He said, "But there isn't one!" and I said. "That's classy!"

It is an honor to be asked to be a best man as well as terrifying. But the groom promises me that if I do a good job I can be the best man at his next wedding.

Of course, we've all heard about people getting cold feet before a wedding, but I've got to tell you, up until this moment I wasn't sure I was actually going to make it. Two words, "World Cup."

Actually, the only reason I accepted the job was for me to make fun of the groom. Let me start by saying that I think I know him better than anyone else in this room, even his parents, because there are a lot of extremely embarrassing things he's done that he has never told his parents. I just happened to bring a list of them. *[Bring out list]* Just kidding, I wouldn't do that to you.

I've got plenty of stories, but the unfortunate thing is not one of them would be appropriate for the occasion. However, my memory tends to improve with alcohol, so if you catch me in the bar later, you never know what I might remember. Anyway, for those of you present that might not know the groom as well, I will try to give you a potted history of the man himself.

He was born in April 1976, a significant year that not only saw the invention of the first advanced microchip, but also had the hottest summer on record in the U.K., which apparently significantly reduced the I.Q. of all children born that year… apart from me. This was the year that Kermit the frog and Miss Piggy fell in love, it's funny how history repeats itself, isn't it?

We have spent most of our childhood and teenage years growing up together, which has been twenty-five years. I have known the bride for nearly three years and it feels like twenty-five. We went to the same school, so I'm able to tell you he was an ideal pupil that excelled in most subjects. Sorry I meant to say he was an idle pupil that was expelled from most subjects.

He didn't spend too much time studying, most of his time he spent playing soccer, playing on his computer, and his favorite pastime which was chasing young women. He pursued girls before I did, and this has had great bearing on his life. He will probably tell you that he went into the travel and tourism industry to see the world and expand his horizons, but the only reason he chose that occupation was that it was full of girls.

I know it's also traditional for the best man to mention the number of ex-girlfriends that the groom has had. But I don't want to get into all that, I think it's vulgar and offensive to the bride. But, suffice to say, sixty-three turned out to be your lucky number after all.

Anyway, through his great effort and luck he met the girl of his dreams in this occupation, and when this happened he promptly found another occupation, job done!

If there was one thing that I was certain of it was that he was going to get married, as he's always been a bit of a love bird. But I recall years ago him saying that he would never marry, but if he did he would marry a woman with small feet. "Why small feet?" I asked, " So she can get closer to the sink," he answered.

Enough jokes. It is an honor for me to be the best man. He is the closest friend and cousin I'll ever have, and it would be fair to say we are like brothers. I remember when I dropped out at university, he was there, all the times I used to get in bother… he was there. When I broke my arm at school he was there, when I was bitten by an Alsatian dog he was there. In fact, thinking about it, you are a bit of a jinx.

I have always wanted the best for him. I know when he met the bride and told me about her, it soon became obvious that she was the one for him. I recall talking to her when we were first introduced, she told me that the first time she laid eyes on him she thought that he was handsome from afar, but now she tells me, she thinks he's far from handsome.

You have to give credit to them in that they have been very wise in the timing of their engagement because long engagements give people the opportunity of finding out each other's character before marriage, which is never advisable. I just hope that she will get used to his farting habits, saying that every time I've stayed at their place I have discovered that it's a joint habit, it's a match made in heaven.

I know that they share the same core values and principles and I am sure that their relationship will continue to grow. He told me that he thinks of her often when he is away from her, especially when he's playing on his computer—he's romantic isn't he? Anyway, I know that no other woman has ever made such an impression.

This is the happiest day of your life, well at least that's what the bride told me earlier, and so it should be, for you have just married a most beautiful, humorous and successful woman and you have married… this.

And now to the cards:

[Read out cards, plus the following]

We have tried the groom in every position and found him to be useless in all of them. Hope you have more luck than us.

All the best, from the soccer team.

Fax from the White Rock Hotel in Kefalonia (the honeymoon location):

Congratulations to you both on this special day. We very much look forward to making your stay a special and memorable one. Don't worry if there is some delay on your arrival, we are putting something on for you—the roof.

You are an excellent friend and a cousin and it has truly been an honor being your best man. The bride is a lovely person, she deserves a good husband, and it looks to me as if she has found one in you.

I'm sure I speak for all the guests here today in giving thanks to the parents as well as the happy couple, for organizing and providing a great wedding and great food.

On behalf of the bride and groom I would like to thank everyone here for sharing their day, particularly those of you who have traveled long distances. I started planning this speech six months ago, and you must feel like I have been delivering it equally as long, but now it gives me immense pleasure, not to mention relief, to invite you all to stand and raise your glasses in a toast to the bride and groom. We wish them well for the future and hope they enjoy a long and happy marriage.

Best Man Speech – Example 10

The following speech was written, delivered by, and reproduced with the kind permission of Lee Sporle and Andy Broderick.

It's another "dual" best man speech and it is a very good one. Lee and Andy have made use of props all the way through the speech and this tends to work for two reasons. Firstly, using props that are placed on the tables makes the guests feel involved in the speech. Secondly, props add visual humor, which greatly enhances the speech.

Best man 1: When starting to prepare what I was going to say, I referred to one of the many books that I have, especially the sayings and philosophy of that wise man Confucius. Confucius says: "The best man's speech lasts as long as it takes the groom to make love." Ladies and gentlemen, thank you very much.

We are very honored to be doing this job. The company is excellent; the hospitality couldn't be better; we have a beautiful bride to admire; and there is an evening of partying ahead of us. In time honored best man tradition I will now do my best to give the groom the most uncomfortable five minutes of his life. Which to be fair is only what he gives the bride everytime they go to bed.

Best man 2: If you would like to open envelope one on your table. *[Photo of groom as a baby]* On December 15, 1968 a baby boy was born, just in time for the opening at the local bar. He was born weighing in at 8 lbs and 10oz, and looking at him today he may have gained a few pounds!

Best man 1: It was clear from an early age that the groom was mad on cars. As we grew up together his cars were always big projects and the most memorable car for me was his Hillman Imp, which he turned into a rally car for one special event. I was the lucky co-driver in this event and on one high speed corner we ended up in a plough field. He was very concerned about his car. I was more concerned that I had lost my pencil and notes and we wouldn't find our way home. Sod the notes and pencil were his remarks, what about my car! If you would like to open envelope two. *[Photo of car]*

Best man 2: He went through what can only be described as an "experimental" stage of his life. If you would like to open envelope three on your table, which as you can see involved dressing up! *[Photo of groom dressed as woman]* Any opportunity to dress up, such as a fancy dress party, no matter what the theme was, or even going to the corner shop for a newspaper, would be a good enough excuse to dress up.

Best man 1: When we traveled Australia we were obviously in a very hot climate. Shorts and T-shirts the norm. He always had to go one further and when someone said to him, "Shall we go into the bush mate?" he took it quite literally. If you would like to open envelope four on your table you will find out. *[Photo of Aussie Outback]*

Best man 2: If you would like to open envelope five on your table. *[Photo of groom and baby]* On August 27, 1997 the bride and groom became proud parents of a lovely boy. But as you have seen from the previous photos, and heard from the stories today, it was obviously a miracle that he became a father! So much so that we were wondering if the bride's real name was Mary Magdalene?

Best man 1: *[Best man 2 to hand groom tools]* It got to the stage where cars were just not enough of a project for the groom, he needed more. "I know I will buy a house, completely gut it and rebuild it from scratch," he said. Two lengths of two by four, six bags of four-inch crosshead screws, one claw hammer, and fifteen months later the groom can literally build you a house, and notice I didn't say he needed a level. If you would like to open envelope six on your table. *[Photo of house]*

Ladies and gentlemen at this point we would like to make a toast to the bride and groom. May the roof above you never fall in and may you both never fall out.

Best man 1: If you would like to open envelope seven on your table you will see we are at the present day, and what a wonderful couple they make. *[Photo of bride and groom]* I'm pretty sure that the groom is glad the best man speeches are after the wedding and not before!

Best man 2: When we were waiting at the church today I asked the bride's mom about some stories from her childhood. She said that when the bride was a toddler, she remembers sending her to bed with a dummy. Funny how history repeats itself.

I did some research and came across an ancient book with a number of definitions regarding marriage: It said:

* The aisle: It's the longest walk you'll ever take.
* The altar: The place where two become one.
* The hymn: The celebration of the marriage.

I think Lisa must have read the same book because as she came up the aisle, I'm sure I heard her whispering: "Aisle, Altar, Hymn, Aisle, Altar, Hymn."

Best man 1: *[To the bride]* We wanted you to know how wonderful you looked today and we asked some of the people here today to give you a vote by means of scorecards. So would everyone please hold up your cards. Guys please turn them up the other way! Wow! *[Photos of the bride]* You didn't really think you were going to escape. Here are some of your finer moments. If you would like to open the last envelope.

We also sought some professional advice for you on marriage and we took a few pointers from the *Good Wife's Guide*:

Best man 2: Prepare yourself: Take fifteen minutes to rest so you'll be refreshed when he arrives. Touch up your make-up, put a ribbon in your hair, and be fresh-looking. He has just been with a lot of work weary people. *[Present the bride with a ribbon]*

Best man 1: Your Goal: Try to make your home a place of peace, order, and tranquillity where your husband can renew himself in body and spirit. Don't greet him with your problems. Don't complain if he's late for dinner or even if he stays out all night. Count this as minor compared with what he might have gone through that day.

Best man 2: Remember, he is master of the house. You have no right to question him.

Best man 1: We also asked some of the men here today what rules they wish woman knew. Here are a few: Shopping is not a sport.

Best man 2: Anyone can buy condoms.

Best man 1: No we don't know what day it is. We never will. Mark anniversaries on a calendar.

Best man 2: Sunday equals any sport. It's like the full moon or changing of the tides. Let it be.

Best man 1: Please say whatever you have to say during commercials.

Best man 2: Don't fake it, we'd rather be ineffective than deceived. We tried to ask some of the groom's ex-girlfriends for some advice for the bride. However, due to the outbreak of a sheep epidemic there are not many left.

One last piece of advice from me: It's important to get on with your mother-in-law. I didn't speak to mine for two years! It's not that I didn't like her, it's just that I didn't like to interrupt!

Best man 1: We would now like to read out the telegrams. The groom's boss said, "Working with the groom is like working with a God. He's rarely seen, he's holier than thou, and if he does any work it's a miracle."

Best man 2: To the bride, "We could have been so good together all the best for the future." George Clooney.

Best man 1: To the groom, "We could have been so good together." Elton John.

Best man 2: I would just like to thank the bridesmaids for firstly performing their role so gracefully, and for looking fantastic throughout the day. I'd also like to congratulate them for doing such a great job in making sure that the bride went against her better judgment and didn't change her mind. Ladies and gentlemen—the bridesmaids.

Best man 1: And now before the final toasts. For those of you who don't know our names. We'll be around later so please do not hesitate to come and introduce yourself. We would like to thank the groom for choosing us to be his best men. It has been a great honor and we have both really enjoyed the privilege.

Best man 2: If you would all like to stand again, raise your glasses, and join us in a toast. Wishing them a long and happy marriage.

Best Man Speech—Example 11

The following speech was written, delivered by, and reproduced with the kind permission of Dan McNulty. This speech is reasonably short but it is very good. The early line about imagining the audience naked is an ideal ice breaker—as long as the audience isn't too prudish!

Ladies and gentlemen. Firstly, on behalf of the bridesmaids and myself, I'd like to thank the groom for his kind words. I know the bridesmaids will agree with me when I say it has been both a privilege and a pleasure to be involved today. I must say that the bridesmaids have done an excellent job in getting the bride to the ceremony on time. They both look absolutely fantastic.

[To the bride] What can I say? You look stunning, the groom is a very lucky guy. *[To the groom]* You scrubbed up nicely too; but I think it's a bit of a cheek that you copied my outfit!

When the groom first asked me to be his best man, I told him that I was deeply honored, but it didn't take long for the feeling of happiness to turn to fear and apprehension. I suddenly remembered the last time I had to stand up in front of a room full of people. I was found guilty and fined.

So for today I thought it best to prepare a few lines and now that I've snorted them I feel much better! Seriously though, I was nervous about making my speech today, so I sought some advise from my dear old father. He told me that the best way to overcome nervousness when making a speech, is to imagine everybody in the audience naked, so if you could all indulge me for a minute or two. *[Look at men and show disgust and look at women and wink]*

Another friend of mine also tried to help me out in writing this speech by telling me about a website he had discovered. You simply type in the date of the groom's birthday, and it gives you a list of famous things that have happened on that day throughout history, simple enough.

The idea is to discover some happy or important events that happened, to try to brighten up the speech.

So I entered August 31, and this is what I got:

Princess Diana died,

Jack the Ripper claims his first victim,

Germany invades Poland.

So I guess the groom is just the latest in a long line of disasters.

Well as I'm sure you all know, it's customary for the best man to tell some embarrassing stories about the groom. The obvious place to start would have to be the stag do. For those of you who don't know, nineteen of us spent the weekend in Amsterdam.

Unfortunately, the law of the stag prevents me from mentioning anything about that, and besides, the groom's solicitor has advised caution until the court case comes up next month. I could also mention ex–girlfriends, but most of them were wiped out during the recent sheep epidemic.

There is one story that springs to mind, renowned among his friends, the Indian restaurant incident. Most of us decided to go for a nice quiet meal one night, sadly the groom decided to drink about ten ciders before we got there. To cut a long story short, he spent most of the evening using the mirrored walls to help him stand up. We then had to drag him over our shoulders, about a mile home. The only words he could manage were "Have you got my wallet?"

We only had to wait six years until the next time we saw him drunk, but I'm sure those who came to Amsterdam will agree it was worth the wait.

I just wanted to say that it's been a privilege to be your best man today, and I'm very honored that you chose me to help you two celebrate the happiest day of your lives. Once again, on behalf of the bride and groom, I would like to thank you all for coming and sharing their special day. It's good to see so many of you here—I'm always amazed by how far some people will travel for a free meal—but, seriously, it's great to see everyone.

Well, I'm going to stop waffling on now and invite you all to stand and raise your glasses and join me in a toast. Ladies and gentlemen, the bride and groom.

Best Man Speech—Example 12

The following speech was written, delivered by and reproduced with the kind permission of Iain Norton. As a best man, you would be delighted if you had as many funny stories to tell about the groom as Iain did in this speech. No doubt some of these stories were slightly exaggerated, however poetic licence is part of being a best man. The story about the groom's fondness for fireworks is the best, providing the speaker with some excellent material and the audience with an interesting insight into the groom's character.

" Good afternoon everybody, on about the only serious note of this speech, I would just like to say what an honor it is to be chosen to be best man today, and what an even bigger honor it has been to be the groom's friend over the last few years. How he convinced the bride to let me do this is beyond me, and I feel safe in saying that this is the last time you will ever have your own way, so make the most of it!

[To the bride] Try to relax. Although you are expecting this speech to be full of sexual innuendo, it isn't. It was at first, but my wife caught me trying to put it in, and made me whip it out before I got the chance.

Soon after Tony had told me that he was going to get married, he asked me how much it had cost me to do the same. So I told him, " I have no idea. I'm still paying for it." I explained to him that I had never known what true happiness was until I had got married, but by then it was too late.

Right then, on to a history of the man himself. Some friends of ours suggested that some big nose jokes would be funny here, but I decided that this was cruel and immature. And if I had put any of that sort of joke in, the groom would've sniffed them out ages ago.

He was born on October 8, 1973, and came prematurely. At least he started as he meant to go on. I typed his birthday into an Internet search, and was surprised to discover that during the month he was born, there was a massive increase in U.F.O. sightings all over the world, except for a few dates, one of which was the 8th. Now I'm not saying you were an ugly baby, but anybody that can keep an alien invasion at bay has certainly got something unusual. I would just like to take this opportunity to let my wife know that this was what I was looking at on the Internet whenever I went to bed late.

Then on to school. I hadn't met the groom by this point, and most of the stories he has told me about his school days would land me in a whole world of trouble, should I tell them here, so I won't. I'll tell them over at the bar later. However, he did tell me about all the time he spent behind the bike sheds, perfecting his kissing technique, and without wanting to go into too much detail, generally experimenting. Soon the time came for him to leave that boys' boarding school, and start again from scratch, this time with girls.

He then moved away from home, and came to a decent part of the country, so that he could complete a course in illustration, and it was there that our paths finally crossed. With one of his best chat-up lines that he had learned from boarding school, he sauntered over to me, and whispered in my ear, "Alright mate, where are you from then?"

Very soon after this, I discovered his rather unhealthy obsession with fireworks. He couldn't just light them in his garden at night. He had to dismantle them, combine them, tamper with them, tie them together, and generally make them dangerous! The scary thing was that he usually did all this during lunchbreak at college, while sitting at his desk. Which included lighting them at his desk! One particular college explosion I remember was where he had done his usual butchering of a perfectly good rocket, and lit it on his desk. Everybody present was hiding under their drawing boards as the fuse into the pile of gunpowder got shorter and shorter, then as the sparks and the gunpowder became one, we were all met with a rather pathetic "phut" noise. Disappointed, we all climbed out from our makeshift bomb shelters, just in time for the real explosion to take place. The windows almost blew out, an alarm went off, and students from the far end of the building came to see what the hell was going on, only to be met with a room full of white smoke you could barely see through, and several stunned students who were trying to put on innocent faces, while pretending they had no idea what had gone on.

The other funny firework story was when the groom and his mates, all three of them, were driving merrily along, when he decided it would be funny to launch a rocket from the sunroof of his car. And it was funny. As the rocket got jammed in the tiny gap, and filled the car with more of the thick white smoke I had become so familiar with. Looking back, this could have turned into a nasty accident. Had I not wiped the tears of laughter out of my eyes, I could quite easily have crashed.

When it comes to the groom, the stories of being stupid really are endless. I would have to be here for days to be able to tell only half of them, so here are a few very edited highlights of some of the silliest.

The time when, for some unknown reason, you drove your car to the bottom of a lifeboat jetty, and did a three-point turn at the bottom, with a wheel hanging off each side as you moved backward and forward.

The time we went to a fast food restaurant and you were too mean to buy a burger, so you found one that had been left on a table and happily finished it off by eating round the bite-mark.

The time I tied a rope to the back of my motorbike, and towed you along on a skateboard. We got to about 30mph before the groom lost control (of his bowels, as well as the skateboard), and was thrown off, in a style that Barry Sheene would've been proud of, and knocked himself out.

The time you smashed a store sign after a night out, by accident of course, and didn't manage to get very far before the local police arrived. He thought he would outwit the police, and gave them a false name. What he forgot to do was tell his fellow drunken bum, about this foolproof master plan, so when the policeman asked him what his mate's name was, he sang like a canary, and promptly landed the unfortunate groom in a cell for the night.

Moving swiftly on. When I first met him, I would describe him as good-looking, funny, caring, trustworthy, stu,.....st,.. What does that say? I can't read your handwriting. Although saying that, I can, with my hand on my heart, describe the groom as very generous.

An example of this was on a recent day out, where a large group of us went go-karting. From the first race, right through to the last, he let everybody overtake him. There was even an older guy there who was on crutches, but he didn't care and let him glide past. He eventually finished seventeenth, out of seventeen. And all because he thinks about others, before he thinks of himself. It had nothing to do with the fact he was useless.

I asked the bride if there were any decent secrets that she could tell me about him, and she revealed to me that they have pet names for each other. He, believe it or not, is known to the bride as her little "Vacation Boy." Apparently, it's because he's good while he lasts, but she just wishes he was longer. Don't worry, I'm nearly finished…

Most of you here are probably aware that he is the owner of a very successful business, and before we go too far away from the subject of the bride, I'd like to say that I've no doubt in my mind that without the assistance of her, there is no way he would have the small fortune that he does now. He had a large fortune before she started spending it.

There will be times in your married life, when you will look back on today, and just sit for hours, looking longingly at your marriage licence. I can assure you, I have done that very same thing. And I can also assure you that there are no loopholes!

Although I am fully aware that the groom has been looking forward to getting married for ages, I spoke to him earlier this morning and thought for a horrible moment that he was beginning to have second thoughts. He told me that he woke up and began to feel a little queer. I breathed a sigh of relief when he told me he was just nervous! Love between two people is a beautiful thing. Between five, it's fantastic.

You may, or may not, be glad to hear that this is the closing paragraph of the speech. Please remain seated while joining me in a toast to some very important people. I hope you will take my advice, and meet them at some point this evening. I am already in debt to them for some great times, and here's to many more. The bar staff.

Success is getting what you want.

Happiness is wanting what you get.

I know that you both want what you've got.

Please stand, and join me in raising your glasses.

The bride and groom.

Best Man Speech—Example 13

The following speech was written, delivered by, and reproduced with the kind permission of Tony Lanon.

The speech is peppered with one line jokes and one of the reasons for including it is to remind all the best men that it isn't all about making fun of the groom, making fun of yourself is an equally effective way of getting a laugh. The speaker makes good use of visual props too, including a few examples of 1970s clothes.

Good afternoon everyone, I'm sure you'll all admit this has turned out to be a brilliant wedding reception, yet every silver lining has a cloud, and this one is that you have to listen to me. I'd just like to start by thanking everyone on behalf of the bride and groom for sharing their wedding day, particularly those who have traveled long distances.

Personally I wish you'd all stayed at home, because things would have been a damn site easier for me. When I agreed to be the best man it's a responsibility that I didn't take lightly, so I made a checklist: *[Take out checklist]*

1. Bring the checkbook or credit card for payments the groom may have forgotten (or in his case be too mean to pay for).
   [Hold checkbook and credit card so people can see]

2. Help the groom dress. I chose his attire, if he got his way, we would have both been dressed like this: *[Hold up 1970s gear]* flares, tank top, and wide

collared shirt. Look at the size of those flares, I bet there's a few of you out there who actually got married in these.

3. See that any angry ex-girlfriends are kept at bay—I found out, however, that most of them were far from angry, they were all out partying last night.

4. Ensure that the groom:

 a) Uses the toilet before entering the ceremony.

 b) Ties his shoes.

 c) Washes his face and combs his hair, or in his case gelled to perfection.

 d) Cleans his teeth and freshens his breath from garlic.

 e) Does up his fly. Stand up and let's see. *[After inspection say "good man"]*

5. Finally, make a speech at the reception. So I'm not doing too badly so far.

 Firstly, on behalf of the bridesmaid, I'd like to thank the groom for his kind words. I have to agree that she looks absolutely wonderful, and has done an excellent job this afternoon in getting the bride to the ceremony on time, because we all know what her time-keeping is like.

 I would like to congratulate the groom on his impeccable taste in choosing such a beautiful wife, and well done to the bride, on saying "I do" to my mate. I'm sure we all agree that the bride looks absolutely stunning and the groom looks absolutely stunned.

 I have to admit to being a bit nervous about today's speech, especially as it's a family occasion. So bearing that in mind, I've removed all the controversial and offensive material from my speech. [Go to sit down] Ladies and gentlemen thank you very much and goodnight. Only joking, where were we?

The human brain, it's a wonderful thing isn't it? It never stops working from the moment you're born until the day you have to write a best man's speech. *[Pull funny worried looking face or put finger on mouth looking puzzled]*

Anyway, I wanted to be able to offer the happy couple some advice on marriage, however, being a single man, there's not been much call in my life so far to talk about love *[milk the audience's sympathy]* but seeing these two together, so happy and in love, it makes me feel both delighted for them and also green with envy. So if there are any single girls out there, touched by my sensitivity, my telephone number is … Alternatively I'll be drowning my sorrows at the bar later.

But I do think about marriage, I think about it quite often. It's a way of keeping my mind off sex.

Even just having a girlfriend seems to bring trouble. There was one occasion—I'd better be careful here—so I'm not going to mention any names, but anyway we'd been going out with each other for about five months, which is pretty good for me, and then the nagging started: "I want to know your name. I want to know your name." So I've got absolutely no idea what it feels like to be happily married, but, of course, nor do most husbands.

Anyway, I decided to do some research on marriage. And who better to look for advice than my own family who between them have had many successful marriages. My uncle had three, my cousin had two, my aunt had two…

I've been told that getting married is very much like going to a restaurant with friends: you order what you want, then you see what the other guy has and you wish you'd ordered that. A friend of mine bought his wife a new car, she phoned him up on her mobile and said that, "There was water in the carburetor." So my friend asked her where the car was and she replied, "In the lake."

But it was my uncle who used to tell me that you always know when you meet Miss Right. So I said "Well, why did your marriage break down?" He said that he did marry Miss Right and he just didn't know that her first name was Always. In fact, after his honeymoon, he said he didn't speak to her for seven months. Then again, he didn't like to interrupt. But, that's my uncle. In my view, for a healthy marriage, you need a healthy person. I'm surprised how healthy and fit you are, despite the amount of alcohol you seem to consume. Now I do think a healthy person equals a healthy marriage. Take my old gran—when she turned sixty, she gave up smoking and drinking and started walking five miles a day. She's ninety-seven today and God knows where she is.

Getting back to advice, just last week (get newspaper out) I was reading the paper and I came across this advert and it says, "Complete set of encyclopedias for sale, just got married, wife knows everything."

So, what can I say about the groom? I have known him for about six years, since we worked at the same place and we actually used to live round the corner from each other when we were young. We used to share a ride into work together. He often used to ring me and say, "Have you got a spare brick, so that I can reach the pedals in my car because I've lost mine?" I remember the days when he had his old car, complete with swimming pool on the passenger side floor, and I had my old car, quite often we had to give each other jump starts in the morning.

Do you know he once thought of himself as a bit of a car mechanic? He once bought a starter motor, the wrong size I might add, which stayed in his desk at work, until he moved departments. Even then he didn't take it with him. God knows where it is now, but I can often hear new people comment when they open their desk drawer for the first time quoting, "Theres a starter motor in here" at which point he can be seen scuttling across the office toward the exit with a huge smirk on his face.

We all know that the groom is not a big drinker, in fact he's not big in any aspects? *[Look toward the bride]*

Do you know on the first night of his stag do, he actually went to bed early, while the rest of us went out clubbing, until three in the morning, He slept for twelve hours.

Another drinking story which springs to mind, which I believe was either just before or just after he got together with the bride, was when we all went on a company bowling night out, and the groom, having had two or three drinks too many, decided to spray a bottle of cheap champagne all over everyone. Bosses, organisers, you name it, they got sprayed. I don't believe he made it into work the next day, the words "sick" and "bath" spring to mind. But when he got back to work he had to email everyone he had sprayed with a public apology.

What's this? He has a fetish for licking peoples ears when he is drunk, and even putting on aftershave at three in the morning before going to sleep after a night out. Sorry, better not mention the sheep stories.

And now onto the bride. There are six words that describe her perfectly: beautiful, charming, delightful, enchanting, pizza, and wine.

And now for my final words of advise to both bride and groom. *[To the bride]* Men are like fine wine, they start out like grapes, and it's your job to stamp on them until they mature into something that you would like to have dinner with.

[To the groom] Women are also like a fine wine. They will start out fresh, fruity, and intoxicating to the mind, and then turn full bodied until they go all sour and vinegary, and then they give you a headache.

On a more serious note, the groom has been a great friend to me over the years and it has been a great honor to be your best man.

A nicer more perfectly suited couple you could not wish to meet, and I wish them all the happiness in their future together.

Could you please stand now and join me in a toast to the parents of the bride and groom for this special day, and to all those who were sadly unable to be here.

And would you all remain standing again, joining me in a toast to the happy couple. The bride and groom.

Best Man Speech—Example 14

The following speech was written, delivered by, and reproduced with the kind permission of Peter Hart. This speech comes from a best man who is the groom's brother. It was written for a wedding reception which took place in Germany. He includes a familiar joke at the beginning but with a twist to make it more original. His story about the groom's exploits in his uncle's car at a young age is an excellent childhood reminiscence to include and his use of the groom's likes and dislikes provides lots of material for jokes.

Bride, bridegroom, ladies and gentlemen, Guten Tag. When the groom asked me to be his best man I immediately thought that the simplest way to put a speech together was to get one from the Internet.

I started looking at hundreds of ready-made speeches kindly donated by past masters, only to discover that ninety percent of them always start with the same joke—you know the one, being the best man is like making love to the Queen, it's a great honor, but nobody wants to do it, so I thought I wouldn't use it!

The next thing that the website tells you is that it's the best man's job, in his speech, to extol the virtues of the bride and then explain to her all those details about her new man that so far he has carefully avoided telling her. So let me tell you a few things that you may be interested in.

The groom is that older brother who can always talk more, eat more, and stay up later. Following in his footsteps has always been a stretch, even if I had wanted to. As we know, he is highly competitive. I can never forget that he is two and half years ahead of me. Although I wonder why, with such a head start, he hasn't got further. This state of affairs has, however, given me the advantage of being able to watch him. And surprisingly it has not always been his successes, the biggest of which we are here today to witness, but some of his most hideous mistakes that I have been able to learn from. This has not just saved me from being pursued by bank managers all over the world, it has been much more instrumental.

The year is 1953—famous for the Queen's Coronation and of course a notable success for the groom—he was born. I don't think this was a mistake, but you'll have to check with my parents afterwards for the real answer.

He soon became a well known face in his local town (and not just with the police) but also with friends and family. At the age of five he got to know the back of his great uncle's hand very well. This was when he thought that the minimum age for driving a car had been substantially lowered. His aunt and uncle were over for tea and a gleaming black car was parked outside the house. He couldn't resist seeing what would happen if you released that funny-looking handle. Both of us were in the car that day, which suddenly gathered speed and headed-off down the road only to be stopped in its tracks rather forcefully by a neighbor's tree. Not known for his athleticism and gymnastic ability, that day proved that if you have sufficient will and motivation, then

Olympic Gold in running can be within anyone's grasp. Sadly, for his bottom, the car became part of the tree and his uncle, having left his mark, never visited again.

He progressed through life and school where he became interested in chemistry. One day he decided to experiment with some materials (sadly for him Viagra was still to be invented) that someone had foolishly given him as a present in a chemistry set. Like most children he decided to make something that would make a loud bang, only he decided to do this in our greenhouse. Later that day, when the greenhouse no longer had any windows, he decided that perhaps medicine would be a safer option.

He charmed his way through the rest of his school days. Some say it was bribery, but anyway he became head boy and got himself a free trip to Canada as a Rhodes Scholar. Then the world of medicine was waiting for him. He worked very hard to become a doctor, although a lot of the time we all thought he wanted to be a butcher as he always stayed on late to cut up those extra portions on the bodies and he always explained the intricate details to the rest of the family at suppertime. Then, of course, there was all that extra revision that he needed to do, especially the practical examinations which, conveniently, only the nurses could help with.

So he qualified—ages ago, it seems—actually, it was ages ago. He launched himself on to the world. What happened next is history—so we'll skip a few years to avoid any legal proceedings. This brings us almost up to date, but there are a few other things you should know.

By now, I'm sure you all know that he likes the good things in life. His love of food is almost as great as, well, I think you know this and I've probably said too much about it already.

He loves Mercedes cars—this I think you know too—and he loves traveling, especially in Europe. I think this is because of all the years our parents dragged him around all the major capitals as a child, having to kick his backside for some disagreement or another.

He loves *money*—so I hope you have plenty of it—as he always tells me he hasn't got any. Maybe you'll discover whether it's true about his secret Swiss bank account.

He loves old films, so you will have to sit through many hours of Hollywood classics or British Ealing comedies. (You will find this very useful if you ever take part in any quizzes.) I find that I know the answer to some of the most obscure questions whenever I take part in any. Here's a test for instance. What was the sequel to the 1955 classic, the *Prisoner of Zenda* starring Stewart Grainger? *[Wait for his answer]* That is correct!

He loves uniforms. Strangely I don't remember him as a child dressing up in any outfits of any kind, and yet he loves seeing and being with people in uniforms. I guess that is one reason why he's working here at the base, so *[to the bride]* I hope you've got yours ready. And of course, he loves *women*, I mean *woman*—that's you, definitely, yes definitely! There's much more, but you'll have plenty of time to discover these things as time goes by. I hope this will help you appreciate a little more about him.

So now, turning to the bride. You really are to be congratulated, you have accomplished a lot so far as his partner. Having applied common sense and stability into his chaotic life, I'm sure that you'll continue to do this with confidence—'cos you'll have to. Today, I'm sure everyone will agree that you make a fine couple.

Now at this point I'm supposed, by tradition, to read out any cards that have been sent through to the happy couple. Ah, here's a few already:

"From X in England (name and address withheld). Sorry I can't be with you on your special day, my solicitor will be talking to you soon. I tried to send you a present but the Post Office said that it would be dangerous because the pin may become loose in transit."

"From the Governor of Bedford Jail, Best wishes on your wedding. Your usual place awaits you on your return."

"The Manager of Barclays Bank, I'm not sending you a present. Please could you put a cheque in the post."

So finally, ladies and gentlemen, please charge your glasses for a toast to the happy couple. I would like to wish you both all good wishes and the best of luck.

Ladies and gentlemen, please be upstanding. in a toast to the bride and groom.

Best Woman Speech

The following speech was written, delivered by, and reproduced with the kind permission of Bhavisha Mistry. It is a "best woman" speech and is comparable to any of the best man speeches.

A wedding provides an excellent opportunity for passing on a few words of advice to a good friend, whether you are male or female.

" Good evening ladies and gentlemen. Firstly, on behalf of the bride and the groom, I would like to thank everyone for sharing this special day with them.

For those of you who don't know me, I am the bride's friend from university. Ever since she told me I had to do a speech, I have been trying to get myself out of it, but now that I have the opportunity and, on behalf of all her friends, little does she know we are about to give her a character assassination! And it will be even more fun now because the groom's already married her and it's too late for him to back out!

Just before I start I'd like to say the bride looked absolutely stunning as for the groom, well he just look stunned!

Those of you who have grown up with her, lived with her, and worked with her, will recognize some of her trademarks. *[To the groom]* No doubt you know all these and remember these have been registered along side your name this morning. Here they are:

Firstly, what she wants she gets. For example, when she first saw the groom perform his camera skills at her brother's wedding, she chased him endlessly even after he expressed he had no interest and now he can't get his hands off her! Secondly, she loves to have tantrums. We all know about those.

Then there's her, my way or no way attitude. You had better watch out, you know who will be wearing the trousers! As for her cooking skills: can cook but won't cook. Lastly, but certainly not the least, she loves her tracksuit bottoms and trainers.

A prime example was this morning after the registry, couldn't wait to get out of her outfit, jumped into her tracksuit bottoms and went downstairs to greet the family, only to be sent up stairs to change into something more appropriate.

Putting the jokes aside, I know that no matter what I say, you have found your Miss Perfect and I know you will love the groom just the same— well you better! Or you will have us girls to answer to!

You've been a great a friend, a good person to go to when you need blunt and straight forward advice, we know not to disagree because we are all scared of you!

Just some advice for the groom:

If you're clever you'll always have the last word, but if you're very clever you won't use it!

Whenever you're wrong! Admit it.

Whenever you're right, shut up!

The bride's spending power doubles, yours doesn't exist!

The best way to remember your anniversary is to forget it just once! Just remember a marriage is made in heaven, but the maintenance work is to be carried out here on earth!

[To the bride] If you could place your hand flat on the table for me please. *[To the groom]* Right, if you would like to place your hand directly on top of hers. Enjoying it? Well, make the most of it because it's the last time you'll have the upper hand!

Now it gives me great pleasure to invite you all to stand and raise your glasses in a toast. To the bride and groom.

To love, laughter, and happily ever after!

From all us girls. Congratulations.

Toasts and Quotes

❦

*W*e generally draw upon life's experiences and the experiences of others when writing a wedding speech and using quotes gives your speech that final polish. When searching for lines and quotes to use, the resources are endless; you can find them here in this section and in other books, magazines, the Internet, television, radio, and even newspapers.

Feel free to adjust the quotes to suit your individual circumstances, but always give credit to the author. If you simply drop in a line taken from someone else and try and pass it off as your own, this will rarely go unnoticed. To cover yourself, precede the quote with an introductory line, such as "While researching for this speech, I came across a quote from…"

Toasting Etiquette

As well as using them in a speech, quotes are great to use while making a toast, as long as they are appropriate. Use a quote that is sincere and don't be afraid of getting sentimental; the guests will probably appreciate this as weddings are quite emotional occasions.

Toasts are offered once all the guests have been served a drink, whether with a meal, or if no meal is served, with the wedding cake. The toasting drink is served to the wedding party in this order: the bride, the groom, the bridesmaids, all other guests at the head table, with the best man last. The only person really required to give a wedding toast is the best man. Be sure that all the guests have a drink before the toasting begins. Toasts can be given at the end of a speech, but the toast is usually offered at the beginning of the wedding meal to welcome everyone and acknowledge the happy couple. The typical order for making a wedding toast is:

1. Best man
2. Father of the groom
3. Father of the bride
4. Groom
5. Bride
6. Friends and relatives
7. Bridesmaids
8. Mother of the groom
9. Mother of the bride
10. Anyone else wishing to toast

Wedding toasts are usually made to the bride or groom individually, the bride and groom as a couple, the bridesmaids, the bride's parents and the guests. If you're being toasted, never raise your glass or drink from it during the toast itself. Always stand and ask others to stand when offering a toast. It's acceptable but not necessary to clink glasses as you raise the toast. Simply raising you glass is fine. The order of making toasts may seem complicated at first, but don't worry it will not be the end of the world if anyone takes their turn out of order.

Tips on Delivering a Toast

Whether the toasting beverage contains alcohol or not, the important thing to remember is that a wedding toast is the one essential ingredient for any wedding reception. It's not to test the drinks for poison, as we are told the Ancient Greeks used to do, but to congratulate the happy couple. Be as creative as you please but make it eloquent. If you feel nervous about giving a toast, remember to keep it simple with just a few short sentences. Follow the tips below to ensure success:

1. Toasts should be kept short (usually four minutes maximum).
2. Never tap the side of your glass with a utensil to get people's attention, you don't want to begin your toast with a broken glass!
3. There's no need to refuse to take part in a toast, if you don't drink alcohol. It is perfectly acceptable to toast with a non-alcoholic drink.

4. A big mistake is to drink too much before you give a toast.

5. Don't joke at the expense of others or use jokes that only a few would understand.

6. Never use swear words.

With a little forethought and preparation your toast will be a memorable addition to the wedding reception. Even though you may feel nervous about making one, make the most of it. You'll find you may even enjoy it and it is a good way of showing that you care.

To the bride and groom
(before the wedding)

Here's to the bride that is to be,

Here's to the groom she'll wed,

May all their troubles be light as bubbles

Or the feathers that make up their bed!

Author— Unknown

To the groom from his bride

I have known many, liked a few, loved only one, I toast to you.

Author—Unknown

To the bride from her groom
(equally suitable for the groom from his bride)

Drink to me only with thine eyes,

And I will pledge with mine;

Or leave a kiss within the cup,

And I'll not look for wine.

Author—Ben Jonson

May I see you gray

And combing your grandchildren's hair.

Author—Unknown

Grow old with me!

The best is yet to be,

The last of life,

For which, the first is made.

Author—Robert Browning

If love makes the world go round,

Then you make it spin.

Author—Unknown

Wherever I roam, whatever realms I see,

My heart untravelled fondly turns to thee.

Author—Oliver Goldsmith

Because I love you truly,

Because you love me, too,

My very greatest happiness

Is sharing life with you.

Author—Unknown

Every day you look lovelier and lovelier, and today you look like tomorrow.

Author—Unknown

A thing of beauty is a joy forever. Here's to you, my beautiful bride.

Author—John Keats

Were't the last drop in the well,
An I gasp'd upon the brink,
Ere my fainting spirit fell,
'Tis to thee that I would drink.
Author—Lord Byron

The world is happy and colorful,
And life itself is new.
And I am very grateful for
The friend I found in you.
Author— Unknown

Never above you. Never below you.
Always beside you.
Author—Walter Winchell

Here's to the woman that's good and sweet,

Here's to the woman that's true,

Here's to the woman that rules my heart,

In other words, here's to you.

Author—Unknown

To my bride: she knows all about me and loves me just the same.

Author—Unknown

Here's to the prettiest, here's to the wittiest,

Here's to the truest of all who are true,

Here's to the neatest one, here's to the sweetest one,

Here's to them, all in one—here's to you.

Author—Unknown

Let's drink to love, which is nothing—unless it's divided by two.

Author—Unknown

I love you more than yesterday and less than tomorrow.

Author—Unknown

To the wings of love:
May they never lose a feather,
But soar up to the sky above,
And last and last forever.

Author—Unknown

Here's to my mother-in-law's daughter,

Here's to her father-in-law's son;

Here's to the vows we've just taken,

And the life we've just begun.

Author—Unknown

To the bride from someone other than the groom

Love, be true to her;

Life, be dear to her;

Health, stay close to her;

Joy, draw near to her;

Fortune, find what you can do for her,

Search your treasure-house through and through for her,

Follow her footsteps the wide world over—

And keep her husband always her lover.

Author—Unknown

Men…

If you kiss him, you are easy

If you don't, you are frigid

If you praise him, he thinks you are fake

If you don't, he thinks you are ungrateful

If you agree to all his likes, you are submissive

If you don't, you are controling

If you visit him often, he thinks you're desperate

If you don't, he thinks you're not interested

If you are well dressed, he says you are vain

If you don't, you are a dog

If you are jealous, he say's you're possessive

If you're not, then he fools around

If you attempt a romance, he say's you are cheap

If you don't, he thinks you are cold

If you are a minute late, he says you are fussy

If he is late, he says you're impatient

If you visit another man, you are fooling around

If he is visited by another woman, "oh we're just friends"

If you kiss him once in a while, he says you're too shy

If you kiss him often, he says you're too forward

If he fails to help you in crossing the street, he brings up the feminist

movement

If he does, he expects to be rewarded

If you stare at another woman, he says you're jealous

If he is stared at by other men, boy, you're in big trouble…

If you talk, it's always too much

If you listen, it's never enough

In short:

So complex, yet so predictable

So macho, yet so sensitive (usually to their own feelings)

So confusing, yet so funny

but most of all,

So irritating, yet so irresistible

…MEN!

Author—Unknown

Here's to the bride. May your hours of joy be as numerous as the petals of

your bridal bouquet.

Author—Anna Lewis

To the groom from someone other than the bride

To the man who has conquered the bride's heart, and her mother's.

Author—Unknown

Here's to the groom, a man who keeps his head though he loses his heart.

Author—Unknown

A toast to the groom—and discretion to his bachelor friends.

Author—Unknown

Marriage has teeth, and him bit very hot.

Jamaican proverb

Women…

If you kiss her, you are not a gentleman

If you don't, you are not a man

If you praise her, she thinks you are lying

If you don't, you are good for nothing

If you agree to all her likes, you are a wimp

If you don't, you are not understanding

If you visit her often, she thinks it is boring

If you don't, she accuses you of double-crossing

If you are well dressed, she says you are a playboy

If you don't, you are a dull boy

If you are jealous, she says it's bad

If you don't, she thinks you do not love her

If you attempt a romance, she says you didn't respect her

If you don't, she thinks you do not like her

If you are a minute late, she complains it's hard to wait

If she is late, she says that's a girl's way

If you visit another man, you're not putting in "quality time"

If she is visited by another woman, "oh it's natural, we are girls"

If you kiss her once in a while, she professes you are cold

If you kiss her often, she yells that you are taking advantage

If you fail to help her in crossing the street, you lack ethics

If you do, she thinks it's just one of men's tactics for seduction

If you stare at another woman, she accuses you of flirting

If she is stared at by other men, she says that they are just admiring

If you talk, she wants you to listen

If you listen, she wants you to talk

In short:

So simple, yet so complex

So weak, yet so powerful

So confusing, yet so desirable

So damning, yet so wonderful...

...WOMEN!

Author — Unknown

To the bridesmaids

To every lovely lady bright,

I wish a gallant faithful knight;

To every faithful lover, too,

I wish a trusting lady true.

Sir Walter Scott

A thing of beauty is a joy forever—Here's to these beautiful bridesmaids.

Author—John Keats

I drink to the general joy of the whole table.

Shakespeare, from Macbeth

Here's to women: they're the loveliest flowers that bloom under heaven.

Author—Unknown

I have a dozen healths to drink to these fair ladies.

Shakespeare, from Henry VIII

The ladies, God bless them, may nothing distress them.

Author—Unknown

To the bridesmaids: we admire them for their beauty, respect them for their
intelligence, adore them for their virtues and love them because we can't help it.

Author—Unknown

And nature swears, the lovely dears

Her noblest work she classes, O;

Her 'prentice hand she tried on man,

And then she made the lasses, O.

Author—Robert Burns

To the newlyweds

As you slide down the bannister of life,

May the splinters never point the wrong way.

Author—Unknown

May your right hand always

Be stretched out in friendship

And never in want.

Author—Unknown

A health to you,

A wealth to you,

And the best that life can give to you.

May fortune still be kind to you,

And happiness be true to you,

And life be long and good to you,

Is the toast of all your friends to you.

Author — Unknown

May the joys of today

Be those of tomorrow.

The goblets of life

Hold no dregs of sorrow.

Author—Unknown

Marriage: A community consisting of a master, a mistress, and two slaves—
making in all, two.

Author—Ambrose Bierce

To the newlyweds: May "for better or worse" be far better than worse.

Author—Unknown

There is nothing nobler or more admirable than when two people who see eye
to eye keep house as man and wife, confounding their enemies and delighting
their friends.

Homer, Odyssey

May your glasses be ever full.

May the roof over your heads be always strong.

And may you be in heaven half an hour

before the devil knows you're dead.

Author—Unknown

May there always be work for your hands to do.

May your purse always hold a coin or two.

May the sun always shine warm on your windowpane.

May a rainbow be certain to follow each rain.

May the hand of a friend always be near you.

And may God fill your hearts with gladness to cheer you.

Author—Unknown

May you grow old on one pillow

Armenian toast

Two such as you with such a master speed

Cannot be parted nor be swept away

From one another once you are agreed

That life is only life forevermore

Together wing to wing and oar to oar

Author—Robert Frost

It's still the same old story,

A fight for love and glory,

A case of do or die!

The world will always welcome lovers

As time goes by

From the song "As Time Goes By" by Herman Hupfeld.

The meeting of two personalities is like the contact of two chemical substances; if there is any reaction, both are transformed.

Author—Carl Jung

Love does not consist in gazing at each other, but in looking outward in the same direction.

Author—Antoine de Saint-Exupery

Here's to marriage, that happy estate that resembles a pair of scissors; "So joined that they cannot be separated, often moving in opposite directions, yet punishing anyone who comes between them."

Author—Sydney Smith

Here's to the new husband

And here's to the new wife

May they remain lovers

For all of life

Author—Unknown

Let us toast the health of the bride;

Let us toast the health of the groom,

Let us toast the person that tied;

Let us toast every guest in the room.

Author—Unknown

May we all live to be present at their Golden Wedding.

May your love be as endless as your wedding rings.

Author—Unknown

May the saints protect you

And sorrow neglect you

And bad luck to the one

That doesn't respect you

Author—Unknown

May you have many children

and may they grow mature in taste

and healthy in color

and as sought after

as the contents of the glass.

Irish toast

May your wedding days be few and your anniversaries many.

Author—Unknown

May your voyage through life be as happy and as free as the dancing waves on

the deep blue sea

Author—Unknown

Here's to the groom with bride so fair,

And here's to the bride with groom so rare!

Author—Unknown

Here's to marriage: one soul in two bodies.

Author—Unknown

May thy life be long and happy,

Thy cares and sorrows few;

And the many friends around thee

Prove faithful, fond and true.

Author—Unknown

Lack nothing: be merry.

Shakespeare, from Henry IV

Heaven give you many, many merry days!

Shakespeare, from The Merry Wives of Windsor

May "a flock of blessings light upon thy back."

Shakespeare, from Romeo and Juliet

Appendix

I f you decide to incorporate certain years from the bride or groom's life with events that happened in that year, the following useful information will give you a general taster of some key events. You will probably find that you have to do much more research to uncover something relevant to your speech, but this should at least give you a starting point. It lists events from 1961 to 1990.

To illustrate this, I was born in 1968 and lived very close to Heathrow airport for the first twenty-five years of my life. My best man made reference to this in his speech and went on to point out that it was in 1968 that the Concorde prototype was first designed and tested. With that he held up a photograph of Concorde along with a profile photograph of me. As my nose is slightly larger than average he commented that I may well have provided the Concorde designers and engineers with their first idea for the shape of the aircraft. A pretty weak line in my opinion (maybe I'm just bitter) but it seemed to go down well with the audience.

Year events

1961

* Eddie Murphy is born.
* Diana Spencer is born.
* Weight Watchers is founded in the U.S.A.
* The oral contraceptive is launched in the U.S.A.
* In-flight movies are introduced by T.W.A.
* Bob Dylan plays his first gig in New York.
* E-Type Jaguar launched.

1962

* Tom Cruise is born.
* Cans that can be opened with tabs are invented by the City Beer Company.
* Decca records turns down signing the Beatles.
* Marilyn Monroe dies.
* Sean Connery lands the role of James Bond.
* John Glenn is the first American to orbit the Earth.

1963

* George Michael is born.
* The "hover" lawnmower by Flymo is invented.
* The first nude screen tests are held.
* President Kennedy killed in Dallas.
* The Great Train Robbery takes place in England.
* The equal pay law for men and women is passed in the U.S.A.

1964

* Prince Edward is born to Queen Elizabeth II.
* Nelson Mandela sentenced to life for treason.
* Martin Luther King Wins Nobel Peace Prize.
* Arnold Palmer Wins Fourth Masters Golf Title.
* Cassius Clay beats Sonny Liston for boxing heavy weight title.
* Average house price in the UK is £3,360.
* Average weekly wage in the UK is £16 14s 11d.

* Hit songs of this year included Animals, "House of the Rising Sun;" Beatles, "A Hard Day's Night;" and Herman's Hermits, "I'm Into Something Good."
* Movies included *Dr. Strangelove*, *Goldfinger* and *Mary Poppins*.

1965

* Malcolm X assassinated in Harlem.
* Soviet Cosmonaut Leonov is "First Man To Float In Space."
* Sir Winston Churchill dies, 1874—1965.
* U.F.O.'s make headlines.
* Music included Righteous Brothers, "You've Lost That Loving Feeling;" Kinks, "Tired of Waiting For You;" and Tom Jones, "It's Not Unusual."
* *The Sound of Music* and *Dr. Zhivago* premiere.
* Cassette tapes are launched by Philips Records.

1966

* A pint of beer in a British pub costs 1'6d.
* England won the football World Cup.
* At the cinema, *A Man for all Seasons;* on TV, *The Monkees* and the original *Batman* series.
* Miniskirts continue to climb (reaching the thighs).
* Model Cindy Crawford was born along with singer Janet Jackson and boxer Mike Tyson.
* U.S. successfully launched the first Lunar Orbiter, which took pictures of both sides of the moon.
* Music included "The Sound of Silence," Simon and Garfunkel; "We Can Work It Out," The Beatles; and "These Boots Are Made for Walkin," Nancy Sinatra.

1967

* June 5 to 10: Israel defeats Egypt, Jordan, and Syria in the Six-day War, afterward occupying Arab land.
* Race riots in American cities accelerate the "flight to the suburbs" by middle-class whites and blacks.

* July 27: The Sexual Offences Act in Britain decriminalizes homosexual acts between consenting males over 21.
* Films include *Bonnie and Clyde*, *Blow Up*, and *In the Heat of the Night*.

1968

* Both Robert Francis Kennedy and Martin Luther King were shot.
* At age 29, Ralph Lauren founds what will become a fashion empire.
* Films include *Yellow Submarine*, *Romeo and Juliet*, *2001: A Space Odyssey*, and *Night of the Living Dead*.
* The Poor People's March on Washington protests the hunger problem in the United States.
* The first cash dispensing machine is installed by First Philadelphia Bank.
* A horse called Red Alligator strode home to victory at the Grand National, carrying a 140lb jockey. The horse's odds started at an amazing 100—1.

* Songs included "Hello Goodbye," The Beatles and "With A Little Help From My Friends," Joe Cocker.

1 9 6 9

* Armstrong becomes the first man on the moon.
* John Lennon and Yoko Ono spend their week-long honeymoon in bed at the Amsterdam Hilton.
* Reggie Kray and his twin brother Ronnie were sentenced to life for murder.
* October 1: Concorde completed its first supersonic flight.
* Judy Garland dies, aged 47.
* Prince Charles is invested as Prince of Wales.

1 9 7 0

* Paul McCartney leaves the Beatles and issues a High Court writ to dissolve them.

* First Boeing 747 jet lands at Heathrow.
* Brazil wins the 1970 World Cup, captained by Pele.
* Joe Frazier wins World Heavyweight Boxing championship when he beats Jimmy Ellis.
* Hit songs of this year included "Tears of a Clown," Smokey Robinson and the Miracles, and "Bridge Over Troubled Water," Simon & Garfunkel.
* President Richard Nixon has a secret meeting with Elvis Presley.
* IBM launched floppy disks.

1971

* America's most wanted serial killer, Charles Manson, was finally brought to justice for the murder of actress Sharon Tate, the wife of Roman Polanski.
* Apollo 14's mission to the moon.
* Walt Disney World opens to the public.
* Intel launches first Microprocessor.
* Australian, J. D. Newcombe is Wimbledon's Mens' Singles Champion for the third time.

* In the UK, the average price for a house in 1971 was £5,632.
* Hit songs of this year included "Maggie May," Rod Stewart; "Ain't No Sunshine," Bill Withers; and "Rainy Days and Mondays," Carpenters.
* The V.C.R. was launched by Philips.

1972

* February: "Black-outs" are imposed in Britain due to coal shortage.
* Watergate charges are brought against Nixon aides.
* U.S. swimmer Mark Spitz wins five gold medals in Munich Olympic games.
* Coca-Cola sued an entrepreneur who altered the classic T-shirt featuring the Coca-Cola logo to read "Enjoy Cocaine." On a similar note, a man wearing a T-shirt promoting a gay "hunky man" contest made the news when he was allegedly made to turn his shirt inside-out to enter Disneyland.

* Hit songs included "I'd Like To Teach The World To Sing," The New Seekers; "Puppy Love," Donny Osmond; and "My Ding-A-Ling," Chuck Berry.
* Just as people were starting to get used to dodging Space Hoppers on the streets, roller skates arrived to put the fear of God back into pedestrians everywhere.

1973

* The United States, North and South Vietnam, and the Vietcong sign the Paris Agreement, instituting a cease-fire in Indochina.
* Italian film-maker Bernardo Bertolucci makes *Last Tango in Paris*, which is controversial because of its explicit sex scenes.
* British psychedelic pop group Pink Floyd releases *Dark Side of the Moon*.

1974

* February and October: Prime Minister of Britain, Harold Wilson, was victorious in not just one, but two General Elections.
* Abba won the Eurovision song contest with their song "Waterloo."
* *The Godfather—Part II* was released.
* West Germany beat Holland 2—1 in the world cup final.
* Disposable plastic razors invented by Gillette.
* Scientists prove that C.F.C.'s destroy the ozone layer.
* Songs of this year included "Gonna Make You a Star," David Essex; "When Will I See You Again," Three Degrees; and "Billy Don't Be a Hero," Paper Lace.

1975

* Women living in Britain were finally entitled to equal pay.
* The first kidney transplant was televised and dog spectacles were patented.
* Lego was Toy of the Year for the second year running.
* The wedge-shaped Lotus Esprit was launched.
* A seven-minute rock opera complete with visuals gave Freddie Mercury's Queen their first number one single, "Bohemian Rhapsody."
* The U.K. held its breath as Old Spice, Charlie, and Brut colognes became the sweet smell of success.

1976

* British Labour Prime Minister, Harold Wilson, suddenly resigns, giving no reason. He is succeeded by James Callaghan.

* January 21: The Anglo-French Concorde supersonic airplane makes its first transatlantic flights.
* Apple Computers is founded by Steve Jobs and Steve Wozniak.
* American film-maker Martin Scorsese makes *Taxi Driver*, a violent film about an alienated Vietnam War veteran.
* Alex Haley publishes *Roots*, an account of the family of a black slave who is transported from Africa to the United States.

1977

* Films include two science-fiction blockbusters: George Lucas's *Star Wars* and Steven Spielberg's *Close Encounters of the Third Kind*.
* In Britain, the Sex Pistols' "God Save the Queen" expresses the punk rock movement's feelings during the Silver Jubilee of Queen Elizabeth II.
* Elvis Presley, aged just 42, dies suddenly at home at Graceland in Memphis, Tennessee.

* The U.S. space shuttle prototype "Enterprise" fly's for the first time.
* Virginia Wade won Wimbledon.
* As best supporting actress, Vanessa Redgrave vowed to fight anti-Semitism in her Oscars speech.
* Songs of this year included "Lucile," Kenny Rogers; "The Name of the Game," Abba; and "Silver Lady," David Soul.

1978

* July 25: Louise Brown, the first test-tube baby, is born in Britain.
* 26 October: the World Health Organization announces that smallpox has been eradicated except for small laboratory stocks of the virus.
* A committee of the U.S. House of Representatives concludes that a second gunman was involved in the assassination of President Kennedy in 1963.

1979

* Sony introduces the Walkman radio and cassette player.
* Mother Teresa was awarded the Nobel Prize for Peace.
* Conservative politician Margaret Thatcher becomes the first female Prime Minister of Britain.
* July 16: Saddam Hussein becomes president of Iraq.
* American film-maker Francis Ford Coppola makes *Apocalypse Now*, a vivid account of the Vietnam War.
* Martina Navratilova won the ladies singles at Wimbledon and Bjorn Borg won the men's title.
* Hit songs of the year include "Hit Me With Your Rhythm Stick," Ian Dury And The Blockheads; "Heart Of Glass," Blondie; and "I Will Survive," Gloria Gaynor.

1980

* John Lennon killed by Mark Chapman.
* Ronald Reagan was elected the 40th President of the United States.
* June 30: Six-pences cease to be legal tender in UK.
* July: Bjorn Borg wins fifth straight Wimbledon title; beats John McEnroe.
* The 22nd Olympic Games are held in Moscow, and are boycotted by over 50 nations.
* Hit songs from this year were "Don't Stand So Close To Me" by The Police and "Going Underground" by The Jam.

1981

* Ronald Reagan is shot in the chest in Washington by John Hinckley.
* Marriage of Prince Charles and Lady Diana Spencer at St. Pauls Cathedral.
* McEnroe beats Borg at Wimbledon in men's final.

* M.T.V. is first aired and starts off with Buggles, "Video Killed the Radio Star."
* Compact Discs are introduced.
* Hits of this year included "Imagine, " John Lennon; "Under Pressure," Queen and David Bowie; and "Shaddup Your Face," Joe Dolce.
* Films of this year included *Porkys* and *Chariots of Fire*.

1982

* The Falklands War between Britain and Argentina begins, after Argentinian troops invade the islands on April 2.
* Laker airways collapsed, leaving 6,000 passengers stranded.
* Prince William was born.
* Navratilova and Conners win the Wimbledon singles.
* World Cup final ended Italy 3, West Germany 1.
* Songs of this year were Madness, "House of Fun;" Survivor, "Eye of the Tiger;" and Paul McCartney & Stevie Wonder, "Ebony and Ivory."

1983

* Sally Ride became the first U.S. woman in space.
* The grandson of Alexander Graham Bell answered the first commercial mobile phone call.
* Derby winning horse Shergar was kidnapped—a two million pound ransom was demanded.
* Top hit songs of this year included Michael Jackson, "Billy Jean;" Spandau Ballet, "True;" and Billy Joel, "Uptown Girl."

1984

* The Apple Macintosh computer, with mouse, is marketed.
* American and French scientists independently discover H.I.V., the human immuno-deficient virus responsible for Aids.
* Director James Cameron makes *Terminator*, a film that powerfully portrays a cyborg (half human, half machine), played by Arnold Schwarzenegger.

1985

* The cellular telephone system was launched in Britain.
* Sir Clive Sinclair unveiled his C5.
* Barbie Dolls surpass, in number, the American population!
* England were banned from international football after the riot at the Hysel stadium.
* In Britain, Boris Becker and Martina Navratilova won Wimbledon
* Songs from this year included "Dancing in the Street," David Bowie and Mick Jagger; "Frankie," Sister Sledge; and "I'm Your Man," Wham!

1986

* The Space Shuttle Challenger explodes after launch, killing the crew of seven.
* The U.S. population is 240,113,000.
* Prince Andrew marries Sarah Ferguson.

* Boxer Mike Tyson wins his first heavyweight championship.
* World Cup, Mexico, which Argentina won with the help of the "Hand of God."
* Hits of this year included "West End Girls," Pet Shop Boys; "Chain Reaction," Diana Ross; and "Take My Breath Away," Berlin.

1987

* Bill Gates, co-founder of Microsoft, becomes the first microcomputer billionaire.
* Margaret Thatcher is elected Prime Minister for her third term.
* October 19: Fifty billion pounds was wiped off shares in the London Stock Market after panic on Wall Street in New York as the stock market crashed.
* "Sunflowers" by Vincent van Gogh sells for £24.75 million at Christies.
* The five billionth baby in the world was born in 1987.

* Songs of this year included "Never Gonna Give You Up," Rick Astley; "Nothing's Gonna Stop Us Now," Starship; and "You Win Again," Bee Gees

1988

* Pan Am flight 103 is destroyed by a terrorist bomb over the town of Lockerbie.
* George Bush becomes President of the U.S.A.
* The Duke and Duchess of York announce the birth of their first child, Beatrice.
* Salman Rushdie published his *Satanic Verses* to much controversy.
* British pubs introduced all-day opening to the delight of drinkers everywhere.
* Ben Johnson loses his Olympic gold in Seoul after a positive drugs test.
* Hit songs of the year were "One Moment in Time," Whitney Houston; "I Should Be So Lucky, " Kylie Minogue; and "Nothing's Gonna Change My Love," Glen Medeiros.

1989

* Sky satellite TV was launched in the UK.
* In a night of celebration the Berlin wall is torn down.
* Princess Anne and Captain Mark Phillips announce their separation.
* A massive earthquake hits the San Francisco Bay area minutes before the World Series between the Giants and A's.
* Mike Tyson beat Frank Bruno to retain the World Heavyweight title.
* Hit songs of this year include "Like a Prayer," Madonna; "Back to Life," Soul II Soul; and "Do They Know It's Christmas," Band Aid II.

1990

* Iraq invades Kuwait.
* Microsoft launches Windows 3.0.
* British and French tunnellers linked up their respective sections of the Channel Tunnel.
* World Cup was held in Italy with the overall winners being West Germany.
* Hit songs of this year include "Hangin Tough," New Kids On The Block; "Nothing Compares 2 U," Sinead O'Connor; and "Vogue," Madonna.

Index

Absent guests 20, 23

Anecdotes 22, 35, 130, 159, 184, 196

Appropriate material 29, 31, 181, 204

Best man 7, 9, 10, 13-15, 16, 17, 18,
    20, 21, 22, 24, 70, 72, 99, 125,
    129, 232
    Example speeches 130-203

Best men 164, 175

Best woman 9, 16, 129
    Example speech 201-3

Body language 42, 43-4

Bride 7, 9, 10, 11, 16, 20, 21, 22, 23,
    47, 78, 106-7
    Example speeches 108-19

Bridesmaids 7, 11, 16, 17, 18, 21, 22,
    71, 107, 125
    Example speech 126-8

Brother of the bride 64
    Example speech 64-6

Delivery 31-5, 41, 42, 44-5, 206-7

Drinking 10, 45, 142, 205, 206, 207

End of speech 23, 46, 164

Etiquette 6, 9-18, 204-6

Father of the bride 9, 10, 12, 16, 17,
    24, 47-8
    Example speeches 49-69

Father of the groom 12, 16, 120
    Example speech 121-4

Female speakers 6, 9, 11, 67, 106, 125,
    129, 201

Gifts 20, 35, 70, 71, 107

Groom 7, 9, 10, 11, 16, 18, 20, 21,
    23, 47, 70-71, 118, 125, 129, 130,
    149, 184
    Example speeches 72-105

Hen night 21

Humor 7, 10, 17, 18, 20, 21, 22, 23,
    29, 42, 43, 47, 48, 49, 53, 57, 60,
    70, 72, 78, 83, 90, 94, 109, 125,
    126, 129, 130, 138, 142, 154,
    190, 196

Mother of the bride 12, 17

Mother of the groom 17

Nerves 8, 10, 31, 43, 45, 142, 159,
    206, 207

Offering advice 23, 35, 121, 125, 127
Opening lines 20, 43, 94, 181
Order of speeches 10-11, 16-18,
    120, 205

Practice 28, 32, 41, 43
Preparation 31-5
Presentation 7
Prompt notes 33-5, 43
Public speaking 6, 8

Quotations 7, 49, 53, 112, 121, 125,
    126, 164, 204-31
    Bride and groom 207, 222-31
    Groom, from bride 208
    Bride, from groom 208-14
    Bride, from others 214-16
    Groom, from others 217-19
    Bridesmaids 220-22

Reading telegrams/letters 23, 27
Research 24-7, 232

Sentiment 6, 7, 22, 44, 47, 48, 49, 53,
    78, 83, 106, 121, 126, 130, 145, 204
Significant dates 87, 90, 170, 232-54,
    57, 60
Sister of the bride 67
    Example speech 67-9

Speech scrapbook 24
Stag party 21
Structure of speech 19-23, 35-40
Subject of speech
    Brief biography 149
    Career 26
    College days 26
    Hobbies 26, 57
    Infant years 24-6
    Relationships 27
    School life 26

Timing 13, 16, 29, 32, 33, 42, 70, 87,
    108, 112, 206
Toastmaster 12-13, 14, 15, 17
Toasts 23, 35, 45, 107, 120, 125,
    204-31

Ushers 14, 17

Visual props 7, 26, 30, 60, 130, 142,
    164, 190, 232

Who speaks 9-10